WHAT *You* WEREN'T TOLD About Righteousness

WHAT *You* WEREN'T TOLD About Righteousness

"Don't be a sail boat that is blown about by every wind. Be an oak tree which is firmly planted and will never bend."

David Ramiah

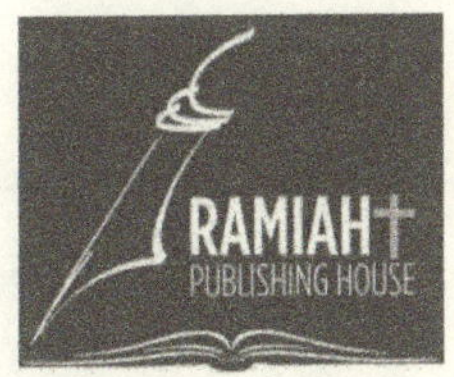

What You Weren't Told About Righteousness

Copyright © 2007 by David Ramiah.

All rights reserved.

Unless otherwise noted, all scripture quotations are taken from the *Holy Bible, King James Version*, Cambridge, 1769. Used by permission. All rights reserved.

Scripture quotations marked "NAS" are taken from the *New American Standard Bible* ®, Copyright © 1960, 1962, 1963, 1968, 1971, 1972, 1973, 1975, 1977, 1995 by The Lockman Foundation. Used by permission. All rights reserved.

No part of this publication may be reproduced, stored in a retrieval system or transmitted in any way by any means, electronic, mechanical, photocopy, recording or otherwise without the prior permission of the author except as provided by USA copyright law.

This book is designed to provide accurate and authoritative information with regard to the subject matter covered. This information is given with the understanding that neither the author nor Christ Exalted Ministries is engaged in rendering legal, professional advice. Since the details of your situation are fact dependent, you should additionally seek the services of a competent professional.

Cover design Lindsay B. Behrens & Daniel Yoshizawa

Published in Canada

ISBN: 978-0-9733247-8-5

12.12.12

Printed in the USA

Previously published 07.01.03 by Tate Publishing Inc. with ISBN:1-6024709-3-6

2nd Printing 19.08.2015

To the loving memory of

ALAN CHRISTOPHER MOHABIR

My cousin died on the 29th of June 2006, two weeks before his twenty first birthday. We thank the Lord for the years that He gave Alan to be with us, and for the joy he brought into our lives. He will never be forgotten, but will be missed.

ACKNOWLEDGMENTS

Thank You Holy Spirit for the privilege and honor of writing this book. You filled me up from the depth of my spirit as I put pen to paper, fingers to keyboard and sights to the vision, and captivated and influenced me to create this marvelous work. I love You.

To my Mom and Dad: thank you for your love and support without which I wouldn't be doing what I do. I love you both very much.

To three guys and one gal who make life a joy: my nephews and my niece; Ryan, Jonathan, Joshua and Briana. I love you.

To my sisters, my brothers and my two sister-in-laws: your love and confidence in me has supported me all the way. I love you. God bless all of you.

To Grandma Liz: there is no one else like you. I love you.

To one very special lady whom I will never forget: Thank you for your hard work of dotting the "I's" and crossing the "T's," and presenting wonderful suggestions. Your great input into this book will never be forgotten!

Thank you "Mrs. Editor" - Mrs. Joy Hallwood. God abundantly bless you.

CONTENTS

INTRODUCTION

I wept many times as Holy Spirit flowed in wisdom, understanding and compassion for humanity while writing this book.

What You Weren't Told About Righteousness will touch you emotionally and awaken your spirit as it connects you with God through the senses. The biblical truth in it is presented in simplicity and in human practicality. You will be placed in an experience with your Maker and not merely be intellectualized.

Common sense demonstrations of biblical facts will effortlessly transform your perception of your status with God. They will bring you into more awareness of righteousness.

You will realize that you remain in that state as long as you continue in right relationship with Him. You can *stop trying to be righteous* and accept the truth that you are already.

There is no longer any need to struggle to be more virtuous so that God might accept you. You are worthy of such a "spiritual" place in Him.

God has revealed that you are already righteous enough according to 2nd Corinthians 5:21. That is why *if you died today you would go directly to be with Him* in Heaven. And it is an act of His that has accomplished this, not yours.

"For it is God who works in you both to will and to do for

His good pleasure." Philippians 2:13

Your part in this must be an "act of faith."

"Don't be a sail boat that is blown about by every wind. Be an oak tree which is firmly planted and will never bend."

As you examine these pages, let the wind of Holy Spirit blow over you and fill you like He filled those present on the day of Pentecost. Let His love flood your soul, and allow His amazing grace to bring you joy.

Give room to Him to destroy the concept and belief of, "I am but filthy rags" deserving nothing from God. Permit Him to demonstrate to you that you are accepted and in right standing with Him in Christ.

The Bible tells us to study to be wise. Even though this book is a deep study, meditate on your Bible. You will be like a tree that is planted by water and you will flourish. Your life will be fruitful.

May the Lord grant you clarity of mind, and may He give light to your understanding to receive and to retain what you are about to learn. *God bless you!*

David Ramiah

Isaiah 52:7, "How beautiful upon the mountains are the feet of him that bringeth good tidings, that publisheth peace; that bringeth good tidings of good, that publisheth salvation; that saith unto Zion, Thy God reigneth!"

Proverbs 3:13, "Happy is the man that findeth wisdom, and the man that getteth understanding."

Chapter 1

THE ACCUSED

"Jesus didn't come for perfect people. He came to make imperfect people perfect."

A full house is gathered. There is a stillness that seems to hold for eternity. Silence cuts through the air.

Everyone is seated facing forward. Eyes are focused straight ahead. It's tense, and like an eerie dawn, it blankets all present. It's a moment most serious. Everyone waits. No one looks around, no one moves, no one speaks . . . Silence . . . Court is in session.

The Prosecutor Satan is the first to proceed. With a step that marches to the beat and rhythm of a director's wand, he step by step presents evidence. He is ready, he is prepared, and he is not going to lessen his effort to see you punished.

Setting out to bring to justice the hardest criminal, he parades up and down from one end to the other. He shrewdly presents significant and key evidence.

Every detail, from the time you were a little child to the present, is brought to the attention of all. He leaves no rock unturned, no trail undiscovered. Every detail is laid out and nothing is left to the imagination. Lastly, he demands the worst punishment.

He then crouches in a corner like a lion that has just captured its prey, licks his chops, and waits for the verdict.

There is silence. A hush engulfs the room. Your head hangs low. Fear grips your heart. You know that you deserve every punishment that might be handed to you. You know that you are guilty of all the accusations. Every detail is true. You did sin, and you are worthy of every penalty for your sins.

You realize that there is nowhere that you could hide. This is it. You are done for. It is time to pay for your deeds. After all, "The wages of sin is death . . ."

Tears flow freely like a stream down your face. Sadness engulfs you. Your heart is heavy. Your knees are weak. There is a knot in your stomach that feels like the size of a melon. And a vision of the lake of everlasting fi re looms in your imagination.

As the enemy of your soul, the accuser of the brethren, hatefully described every detail of your life, there were flashbacks. It was as if you were watching your life pass before you on a television screen. The evidence was there and it made you cringe.

The eyes of those in the courtroom seemed to penetrate the back of your head. You wished that there was somewhere you could run and hide, but you knew there wasn't anywhere.

Feeling Condemned

Unworthiness overwhelms you. Your hands are clammy, your throat dry. The knot in your stomach feels larger now. It is hard to stand. You feel so unclean, so ashamed, so inferior, and so worthy of punishment.

You are still conscious of all eyes on you.

You had listened to the preacher. The messages had touched your heart and you had said a prayer. You had asked Jesus to be your Lord and Savior. But after that, you know that you haven't always obeyed.

There were many times that you failed God. On several occasions you knew to do right, but did wrong anyway. And the thoughts in your head often times were not those of a Christian.

On numerous occasions you went straight ahead, and like a lamb being led to the slaughter you committed sin without restraint. However, every time, by the conviction of the Holy Spirit and His urging, you repented with tears.

Now, you stand before the Maker of your soul, the Judge of all Judges: God Almighty; Creator of the universe, I am that I am, the Most Holy God. Awesome is His Presence and great is His light!

Seated at the right side of Father God is Jesus Christ our Lord and Savior; The Champion of the Universe. He is God of all the earth, the Victorious Warrior.

How could God, so pure and holy, look upon you now? How could He even consider you, someone who was described as such an unclean, wretched, and miserable creature? Described to be so unfit, so filthy, so undeserving; a rogue, a dropout, a reject, a failure, and deserving nothing but hell.

"Will He be merciful to me? Was Jesus' death on the cross sufficient? Was I forgiven all those times that I asked for forgiveness? How angry is God with me right now?"

There seems to be a greater hush in the room. Something seems to be happening. With a stroke of a finger you brush away the tears from your eyes. It is time to face the Judge. You might as well get ready for whatever comes. You lift up your head.

What happens next is not what you anticipated.

Great Love of God

You look up, and your eyes connect and lock with those of the most awesome being in the universe. The eyes that look back at you are like none other, that you have ever looked into. They are brilliantly glistening with love and compassion like you have never known. Love like you have never felt before pierces and overwhelms your soul. It is a look so deep, so powerful, and so intense, it moves your spirit.

You do not understand. How could anyone love you? How could Almighty God, so holy and righteous love someone like you?

But something is happening to you. Those eyes - love so great - compassion without measure; grace in abundance. His gaze is a force so incredible; it holds you up like a rock and causes you to stand firm. Why? You do not understand.

As the gavel struck and rang out throughout the room, He spoke.

With a force that purges and purifies, like rolling thunder, like a roaring gust of wind in a deep canyon, His words rush over you soothing your innermost being. With a gaze that pierces the soul, and with a smile of deepest love and affection, He looks deep into your eyes.

"I, even I, am He that blotteth out thy transgressions for mine own sake . . ." Isaiah 43:25 a

You hear the words and they penetrate your spirit like the sharpest sword. Over and over they orbit your mind.

"Did He say He blots out my sin, for His sake? My sins are erased for His sake? My sins are erased? What does He mean? I do not understand."

Still smiling, He continues, eyes glistening with joy more than that of a father holding his newborn child, ". . . *and (I) will not remember thy sins.*" Isaiah 43:25 b

It is like night and day, dawn from sunrise, morning from evening. One moment you are totally condemned and discriminated against, the next moment you are hearing words that proclaim and indicate freedom.

"How can this be? I am guilty of all of the accusations. I am worthy of punishment. But what is this I am hearing? First I am hearing that my *sins are erased* and now *they are not remembered*. How come? Why?

I must have been forgiven all those times that I repented! The Lord must have answered my prayers every time! But, 'The wages of sin is death . . .' Isn't there some price that I must pay? Why did I always feel so guilty even after I repented? Why did I always feel that it was payback time?"

But He isn't finished. He continues, "Put Me in remembrance: let us plead together: declare thou, that thou mayest be justified." Isaiah 43:26

"He wants me to speak? He wants me to declare? He wants me to plead with Him? Who am I to plead with God? Who am I to declare anything before Almighty God?

He is my Creator and the Creator of the entire world. This is God! This is the Greatest and most Awesome Being in the Universe! Standing here in His presence is astonishing enough, how much more amazing it is to speak or to declare anything in His presence."

Suddenly, you realize that you do not feel the way you felt in the beginning! You no longer feel weak in the knees. You do not feel afraid any more. You do not feel unworthy any longer. You just can't believe it!

"Where has all the guilty feeling gone? Why don't I feel unworthy anymore? Where did all the shame and inferiority go? I do not sense fear. I feel different! I feel new! I feel free!"

Knowledge is Power

We do not realize the great love with which God loves us. We do not understand the length that He went to save us. We do not understand the full extent of what God did for us on the cross through Jesus Christ. If we did, we would not be in the predicament that we are in today.

Most Christians are *struggling daily* with the above scenario. And it is because they do not understand who they are in Christ. Knowing who you are in Christ changes everything.

Jesus said in the book of John, "And ye shall know the truth and the truth will make you free." John 8:32

> Hosea 4:6 says, "My people are destroyed for the lack of knowledge: because thou hast rejected knowledge, I will also reject you . . ."

God is the Great I am that I am. He is the Maker of the Universe. He is God. He is for us who can be against us! He is God who loves without measure. He loves us with a great and unfathomable love that is beyond our understanding and imagination. God is Love!

Jesus did not say that the truth would make you free. He said, "You will *know the truth* and the truth will make you free." It is *when you know truth* that you are made free. Without knowledge of the truth, you remain in bondage to *doubts of what God can and wants to do for you*. Without knowledge you remain in fear of what the enemy could do to you.

When truth is received and Holy Spirit enlightens the understanding, you are released. You are no more in fear of the unknown, of what you didn't know. Knowledge is power.

"The fear of the Lord is the beginning of wisdom: and the knowledge of the holy is understanding." Proverbs 9:10

Knowing that your salvation is a *free gift* from God through Jesus Christ our Lord sets you free. You didn't pay for your salvation. It was given to you without cost. It was given to you because you believed in Jesus Christ and accepted Him as your Lord and Savior.

You believe that He died on a cross for your sins and that He rose again from the dead. You believe that there is power in His blood and that the remission of your sins is in the blood of Jesus.

Your salvation is given to you because of God's grace and because of nothing else. You do not work for it. You cannot buy it. Someone else cannot obtain it for you or give it to you. There is no other way of receiving salvation, but through faith in Jesus Christ.

> "The wages of sin is death; but *the gift* of God is eternal life *through* Jesus Christ our Lord."
>
> Romans 6:23
>
> "That if thou shalt *confess* with thy mouth the Lord Jesus, and shalt *believe in thine heart* that God hath raised Him from the dead, thou shalt be saved. For with the heart man *believeth unto righteousness;* and with the mouth confession is made unto salvation."
> Romans 10: 9, 10

God meant exactly what He said when He said, "*I, even I, am He that blotteth out thy transgressions for mine own sake, and will not remember thy sins.*"

How did He erase our sins?

Debt Paid In Full

God sent Jesus into this world to save us from sin and hell. He sent Jesus to *pay a debt that we couldn't pay.* We owed a debt because we sinned, but *Jesus paid that debt in full.*

The blood of Jesus has redeemed us, and His blood cleanses us of all unrighteousness.

Was God speaking to Israel only when Isaiah wrote the scripture above that He would erase their sins? Yes. However, we have inherited this grace of God through Jesus Christ. We have become the seed of Abraham through inheritance, and thereby received the blessings of Abraham through Him.

> Galatians 3:13,14 says, "Christ hath redeemed us from the curse of the law, being made a curse for us: for it is written, Cursed is everyone that hangeth on a tree (cross): *That the blessing of Abraham might come on the Gentiles (us)*, through Jesus Christ; that we might receive the promise of *the Spirit through faith*."

Paul the Apostle writes in Galatians 3:16, "Now to Abraham and *his seed* was the promise made. He saith not, And to seeds as of many; but as of one, And to *thy seed, which is Christ*."

We became *that seed* being made *the body of Christ*. We became one with Jesus and inherited the blessing of Abraham through Him.

> Paul further shows us this truth in Ephesians 1:22, 23, "And hath put all things under His feet, and gave Him to be the head of all things unto *the church, which is His body . . .*"

Therefore having become the body of Christ, the blessing of Abraham was passed down to us. Therefore the word that God spoke to Israel in Isaiah 43:25 and 26 is now ours also. He is speaking to *children of faith. We are children of faith!* He says to you and I,

"I, even I, am He that blotteth out thy transgressions for mine own sake, and will not remember thy sins."

God is *not going to* blot out our sins, he already has. And He does not remember them anymore. *It is already done.* Jesus said, "*. . . It is finished . . .*" John 19:30.

If you have repented of your sins and received Jesus Christ as your Lord and Savior, your *sins are forgiven* and *also forgotten.* God does not remember your repented sins because He erased them. They are blotted out.

As you stand before Him having been washed by the blood of Jesus, He doesn't see you, He sees Jesus. God only recognizes *the body of Christ.* He does not see sin in the person whose sins were washed by the blood of Christ. *He recognizes righteousness,* His righteousness.

"If we confess our sins, he is faithful and just to forgive our sins, and to cleanse us from all unrighteousness." 1John 1: 9

Captivated

You are standing in awe before Him at His sayings. You finally realize what He is telling you: "Never mind this guy over here on my left, parading up and down as if he owns the place. He can jump up and down, skip and hop, foam at the mouth, rage and carry on, and put forward every kind of evidence he wants to. *He doesn't matter*!

The One on my right hand matters most. What matters most is what He did for you on the cross. What is more important is that you believe in Him and in what He did for you. What He has done for you was done in full. It is finished. It is completely paid. There is nothing left owing. *The debt is paid!* Receive it by faith."

Right then, you catch a glimpse of the Master. His eyes are gleaming and glistening. There is a shy smile on His face and it covers you like a thick blanket on a very cold night. It warms you like an open fi re.

His love knows no bounds as it floods your soul. And the light of His love pushes all darkness out of you as it fills you up with brightness.

You know you are accepted here. You recognize that something great has happened. Without a shadow of a doubt you realize that you are loved beyond measure.

There is an expectation in you that was not there before. Hope surges from the depths of your spirit and fills you up like a well. No more fear or uncertainty clouds your mind. It is like a great breath of fresh air.

You seem alive for the first time. You had this feeling a long time ago, when you received Jesus Christ as your Lord and Savior. But this time, it is greater. There are no doubts.

Liberated

God said to you to declare that you might be justified. He told you to plead with Him, and remind Him. But, remind Him of what?

He obviously wasn't talking about your sins. He has forgotten about them and certainly, they are not what He wants you to remind Him of. What then does He want you to be reminiscent of?

He wants you to be reminiscent of His promises to you. They are many, and they are in His word. He wants you to remind Him that it is written:

> "Verily, verily, I say unto you, he that believeth on me, the works that I do shall he do also; and greater works than these shall he do; because I go unto the Father. And whatsoever ye shall ask in my name, that will I do, that the Father may be glorified in the son. If ye shall ask anything in my name, I will do it." John 14:12–14

> "No weapon that is formed against thee shall prosper; and every tongue that shall rise against thee in judgment thou shalt condemn. This is the heritage of the servants of the Lord, and *their righteousness is of me,*

> saith the Lord." Isaiah 54:17
>
> "Bless the Lord, O my soul and all that is within me, bless His holy name. Bless the Lord, O my soul, and forget not all His benefits: Who *forgiveth all thine iniquities;* who *healeth* all thy diseases. Who *redeemeth* thy life from destruction; who crowneth thee with lovingkindness and tender mercies; Who satisfieth thy mouth with good things; so that thy youth is renewed like the eagle's. The Lord *executeth righteousness* and judgment for all that are oppressed." Psalm 103:1–6

These promises and many others are what God wants you to remind Him of. They are numerous and are found in His Holy Word.

He doesn't want you to remind Him of your sins. He has erased and forgotten them. He doesn't want to be told over and over how weak you are, and how you are full of faults and shortcomings. He doesn't!

God doesn't see you with defects and inadequacies. He doesn't look at you as feeble and powerless. Nor does He recognize you as that *old sinful person* that you used to be. Your heavenly Father does not see failure when He looks at you. He does not perceive you as frail and incapable. He recognizes the Body of Christ, His Son. He sees Jesus.

He sees a new and righteous you: an overcomer; one who can do all things through Christ who strengthens him.

Jesus overcame the world and God recognizes you as one who can overcome the world as well. He perceives a winner, because His Son Jesus is The Winner.

"If we confess our sins, he is faithful and just to forgive our sins, and to cleanse us from all unrighteousness." 1 John 1: 9

If you sinned, but have repented confessing your sins to God, He forgives you those errors and will *cleanse you of all unrighteousness*. That means that there is only one thing that remains, and that is, *righteousness*. You, righteous!

Does this mean that you can go on and continue in sin? "God forbid."

> "What shall we say then? Shall we continue in sin, that grace may abound? *God forbid!* How shall we that are dead to sin, live any longer therein?" Romans 6:1, 2

God forgives and cleanses you of all sin when you repent. But that doesn't mean you are free to continue to live in sin.

Remind God of His promises and not your repented, forgiven, and forgotten sins.

When you do so, it is not for His sake, but for your own. He hasn't forgotten His promises. When you tell Him about His promises written in scripture, *faith will rise up* inside of you. You will be strengthened and encouraged. *You will believe* and receive from God those things that you ask.

"So then faith cometh by hearing, and hearing by the word of God." Romans 10:17

"Therefore I say unto you, what things so ever ye desire, when ye pray, believe that ye receive them, and ye shall have them." Mark 11:24

Chapter 2

THE FATHER

"Recognize God as Father, approach and relate to Him as such. Every day, more and more, you will find yourself in His arms."

Father's Anguish

The sun is setting, and a fresh breeze passes over the land cooling it from the heat of the day. Without the strong glare of a desert sun overhead, he sees a little further than usual.

After taking one last look over the horizon he slowly turns away and saunters back to the house.

Day after day he had hoped that he would see the figure of his son rising over the hill. Perhaps he would see him hurrying along, trying to reach home as quickly as possible. Maybe he will appear on the horizon with arms waving in the air, joyfully acknowledging seeing his father standing there.

That night, he slowly climbs into bed and pulls the covers over his tired body. He tries to sleep. Turning on his side he lays his head on the pillow, and a tear trickles down his face. He slowly wipes it away. A dull aching pain rests on his heart. He misses him so much.

Where is he? Who is he with? Where will he spend the night? Is he safe? Does he have friends who love him and care for him? Is he eating well? Is all well with him? Does he still have money? Does he think of home? Hopefully nothing bad has come to him.

There were many sleepless nights with nightmares of him hurt and dying by the side of a lonely road. There were several evenings that were spent staring in the darkness thinking of him. Many lonely days spent looking over the hill, probing the horizon with longing eyes, and pacing the landscape. Often wanting to go after him, but go where?

Memories of the past resurrected in his heart and flooded his mind. He remembered the times that he had picked him up when he had fallen; the time the boy had run to him crying because he had broken his toy; the time that he came home complaining of his friends not wanting to play with him. He had held him and comforted him.

He remembered the times they had run in the field together playing tag. He recalled the times they caught butterflies together, and the young lad had indicated how beautiful they were. He remembered nights when he had pointed to the stars and told him of their Maker, about the vast open space beyond the clouds, about the angels, heaven and what was in heaven.

"Will I ever see him again?"

> "And he said, a certain man had two sons: And the younger of them said to his father, Father, give me the portion of goods that falleth to me. And he divided unto them his living. And not many days after the younger son gathered all together, and took his journey into a far country, and there wasted his substance with riotous living.
>
> And when he had spent all, there arose a mighty famine in the land; and he began to be in want. And he went and joined himself to a citizen of that country; and he sent him into his fields to feed swine. And he would fain have filled his belly with the husks that the swine did eat: and no man gave unto him.
>
> And when he came to himself, he said, How many hired servants of my father's have bread enough and to spare, and I perish with hunger! I will arise and go to my father, and say to him, Father, I have sinned against heaven and before thee, and am no more worthy to be called thy son: make me as one of thy hired servants. And he arose, and

> came to his father. But when he was yet a great way off, his father saw him, and had compassion, and ran, and fell on his neck, and kissed him." Luke 15:11–20

The days passed by like dark lingering clouds in the sky without a strong wind to blow them on. Increasingly slowly they passed, and he still hadn't returned. His father had waited everyday with deep longing for him to return. Then one day; that glorious day!

Over the hill he came, staggering in the distance. Weak, hungry, ragged and worn, sun scorched, blistered lips, eyes swollen and red. His clothes, torn rags, hung on him like tattered sails on a mast. He was unrecognizable. Yet, he knew him.

Kicking up the sand behind him, falling again and again, he ran to his son. He arrived breathing heavily. Throwing his arms around him, he hugged him. And having great compassion on him, he held him.

The stench of old sweat did not deter his father. The foul odor, from a mouth that had been without proper hygiene for a long time, did not push him away. The pungent pigsty stench did not interrupt their long overdue reunion.

He wasn't concerned about what his son had done or how rebellious he had been. Nor was he preoccupied with the fact that he had squandered all his wealth with people he did not even know, that he had frequented raunchy houses of pleasure and visited with prostitutes.

Not one wrong act, not one bad word, nor any fault or failures of his mattered at that moment. All he was concerned about and all that was important was that his son had returned home. The son that was once lost is found.

He was again in his loving arms and that was all that was necessary. The son whose return he had yearned for; the boy he had held so often and that he loved with all his heart; the boy he had watched grown up to be a young man.

This young man, walking away and disappearing into the world, had left him behind to suffer the lonely agony of a broken heart. Once again, he could feel around him the arms of the son he loved so dearly.

The boy's hot tears fell on his neck and shoulder. His own flowed unhindered as he raised his head towards heaven in gratitude and thanksgiving.

It seemed like eternity while they held each other, neither of them wanting to let go. Finally, they slowly pulled away while still holding each other by the arm.

As they took a long look of affectionate love at each other, laughter of joy burst forth amidst the tears from both father and son. Together again. . . Once more, they embraced.

"I am sorry father, I am sorry," he wept.

"Hush son. Shush, shush, it is not time for that. I love

you. The past is past. We are together again. You are home at last. That is what matters, that is what is important my son," his words breaking up amidst sobs.

"I love you too father," the young man mutters, choking on his words.

"Weeping may endure for a night, but joy cometh in the morning." Psalm 30: 5

The long overdue reunion had finally arrived. Now, after much agony, plenty of sorrow and pain, there is rest. There is joy and there is gladness. Sorrow lasted all night, but joy had come in the morning.

". . . For this thy brother was dead, and is alive again; and was lost, and is found." Luke 15: 32,

God is your Father

God is your Father. He is the Judge of all judges, the Master of the Universe, the Creator of mankind, the Great and Awesome One, God Jehovah. He is loving, compassionate, merciful, kind, true, faithful, and full of grace.

Even though He is God Almighty, He is Father, your Father. And He desires intimate relationship with you. Like the father of the prodigal who bore much pain for his lost son, so too your Heavenly Father bears pain for you.

Throughout scriptures we see evidence of God reaching out to mankind in every way and with every effort. As much as He disciplines, He forgives and receives. We find Him guiding, directing, testing and correcting. Being angry yet forgiving, loving and compassionate, tending, providing and protecting. He is ever watchful and mindful of His children, and always abounding in mercy and grace.

Whenever we read scripture, in whatever light and in whatever mind, we always see one thing. God reaching out to man, time and time again, wanting one thing more than anything else, intimate relationship.

He is a father and as a father He loves His children. Really, nothing else matters to Him. God loves His children, and like any affectionate Father, he wants His children with Him.

He will go to great lengths to get them. He will reach down to the lowest depths. He will climb to the highest heights and search the deepest valleys. He will pay any price. He paid the highest price, the death of His Son, Jesus Christ.

> In Psalm 89: 26 we see that God is our Father,
>
> "He shall cry unto me, Thou art my father, my God and the rock of my salvation." And in Psalm 103: 13 again we see that God is our Father who has compassion on us just like the father of the prodigal who had compassion on his son.
>
> "Like as a father pitieth his children, so the Lord pitieth them that fear him."

Not A School Master

Our knowledge of God is one that depicts Him as a stern old school master. It is of someone, who at every turn waits to discipline us, is ready to whip us, put us to shame, and punish us for every deed. It is of someone who commands us to walk a straight line and if we do not, we can expect punishment.

It is an imagination of a harsh and angry father, who shouts and rails at his children for every little wrong thing they do. It is one of mistrust and fear if we would tell the truth.

This is a mentality of slaves. It is the frame of mind of servants. *God is not seeking for servants or slaves; He is looking for sons and daughters!* We serve Him because we love Him!

We fear God, but not in the way He wants us to. God is not looking for every mistake that we make. He does not look for every wrong that we commit so that He can punish us. Absolutely not! He seeks to bless us.

Moses, Abraham, Isaac, Jacob, David, Solomon, and countless others were blessed beyond measure by God.

You might say to me that these were great men of God and that is why God blessed them. I say to you that they *were forgiven men* of God.

Moses was a murderer, so was David. Abraham did not tell the whole truth about Sarah being his wife. He said she was his sister. Isaac said the same about his wife. Jacob was a conniver and Solomon was a backslider. They were all forgiven men of God.

God blessed others as well who were sometimes not recognized as "great men or great women" of God: the Shunammite woman who fed Elisha; Ruth the Moabitess; Rahab, the harlot of Jericho whom Joshua delivered after the wall fell; and countless others.

These were total strangers not being of the household of Israel. If God blessed strangers, how much more will He bless you, a believer?

When you come to the place of knowing God as your Father, you will relate to Him as Father. You will come to Him as His dear child without doubts or fear. You will approach Him knowing that He is there for you. You will rely on Him completely to provide for you and keep you in perfect peace. You will rest in Him and not worry about a thing.

"All is well with my soul. Nothing bothers me. I do not have a worry in the world."

This is what your Father desires! He wants you to come to Him as a dear child of His. He wishes that you worry about nothing, and He wants you to have peace of mind. He wants you to have security in Him, and to know that all is well with your soul. He desires that you would come to Him as *Abba Father* and to approach Him as *Daddy God*.

Until we come to the place where we see God for who He really is, we cannot completely enter into the unique relationship that He desires for us to have with Him.

> "For as many as are led by the Spirit of God, they are the sons of God. For ye have not received the spirit of bondage again to fear; but ye have received the Spirit of adoption, whereby ye cry Abba, Father. The Spirit itself beareth witness with our spirit that we are the children of God." Romans 8:14–16
>
> "But ye are a chosen generation, a royal priesthood, an holy nation, a peculiar people; that ye should shew forth the praises of Him who hath called you out of darkness into his marvellous light."1 Peter 2:9

Children of God are Kings and Priests. We are of Royal Priesthood, Ambassadors of God, and we are the Body of Christ. But most important of all, we are children, His children. And more than anything else God wants His children to recognize and acknowledge Him as Father.

Jesus' message throughout the gospel stresses the fact that God is our Father and that this is how we should approach Him. He tells us in Matthew 6:6 that when we pray, we should approach Him as "Our Father."

"After this manner therefore pray ye: *Our Father* which art in heaven . . ."

He presses the point further in Matthew 6: 8, ". . . your Father knoweth what things ye have need of, before ye ask him."

Over and over in the gospels Jesus repeated these words, our Father, your Father, and your Father in Heaven. This is because He wants you to recognize not only that God is Creator, Judge, and Master, but equally important He is your Father. Thus, Jesus continually stressed this factual truth throughout His teachings in scriptures: *God is your Father.*

The relationship that God wants with His children is that of a Father and child. The Bible says that Jesus was the first born of many sons. God want sons and daughters. He desires to have His children with Him.

"...That he might be the firstborn among many *brethren.*" Romans 8:29

What does God really want?

He wants to walk and talk with you as He did with Adam and Eve in the Garden. He desires to pick you up when you fall down. He wishes to comfort you when you are sorrowful, to heal you when you are sick, and to carry you when you are unable to go any further on your own.

He wants to wipe away the tears when they flow. He desires to give you peace and joy everlasting. He wishes to bring you into His presence, where you can sit at His feet the same way that Mary sat at the feet of Jesus.

He wants to hold you in His arms and love you. He

desires an intimate relationship with you!

Building Relationship With God

> "And when thou prayest, thou shalt not be as the hypocrites are: for they love to pray standing in the synagogues and in the corners of the streets, that they may be seen of men. Verily I say unto you, they have their reward. But thou, when thou prayest, enter into thy closet, and when thou hast shut thy door, pray to *thy father* which is in secret; and thy father which seeth in secret shall reward thee openly." Matthew 6: 5

Prayer is the key to God's heart. It is communication with God. There, you communicate your needs, wants and desires, your disappointments, hurts and fears, your thankfulness and your praises.

Through this area of communication, relationship is generated and strengthened. Intimacy is built, fortified, and experienced.

Jesus did not teach us to pray *religiously*. That is, going out on to the street corners and praying to show everyone how religious we are, or praying long eloquent prayers before others so that they may see how well we pray.

He teaches us however, to pray intimately, one to one with our loving Father behind closed doors. This is secret prayer between Him and us alone. No fanfare, no displays or demonstrations, just *communicating unceremoniously in faith.*

This is intimate relationship with God. God desires relationship, not customs and traditions or legalistic servitude.

This doesn't mean that you are not to pray in church or in other public places. However, pray always in faith and sincerity.

Share with your Father alone in your prayer room. Communicate with Him your burdens and grief, your needs and wants. And then *give Him the opportunity* to communicate in response to you.

He answers in deliverance and provision. He whispers softly and gently to you, strengthens and comforts you, and He gives you direction and guidance. *Intimate relationship develops and is strengthened between you and Him.*

Requests-Response-Result

Your Heavenly Father desires to give you good things. He will not keep back any good thing from you. He is a Father who wishes to give you the best. Come to Him knowing who He is to you and that He loves you. Remember that He wants the best for you and that He desires to do great and mighty things in your life.

> "Ask and it shall be given unto you; seek and ye shall find; knock, and it shall be opened unto you: For every one that asketh receiveth; and he that seeketh findeth; and to him that knocketh it shall be opened. Or what man is there of you, whom if his son asks bread, will he give him a stone? Or if he ask a fish, will he give him a serpent? If ye then, being evil, know how to give good gifts unto your children, how much more shall *your Father* which is in heaven give good things to them that ask Him?" Matthew 7: 7–11
>
> "He that spared not his Son, but delivered him up for us all, how shall he not with him also freely give us all things?" Romans 8:32
>
> ". . . But they that seek the Lord shall not want any good thing." Psalm 34:10
>
> "For the Lord God is a sun and shield: the Lord will give grace and glory: no good thing will he withhold from them that walk uprightly." Psalm 84: 11

Father is waiting with open arms to receive you, to put a ring on your finger and a robe on your back. He wants to lead you to still waters, to comfort you, to provide for you and to restore your soul.

He desires to fill your cup, to feed you and anoint you with the oil of gladness. He will give you goodness and mercy all your days.

"Call unto me, and I will answer thee, and show thee, great and mighty things, which thou knowest not."

Jeremiah 33: 3

Don't you recognize the heart of your Father as He petitions you to call out to Him? Isn't it because He wishes to do you good and not harm? Isn't it because there is an assurance with the appeal to call? A promise of blessing and that you might see the greatness of your God toward you? And isn't it amazing that God would petition you?

"Call unto me, and I will answer thee," says your Father. He answers every call.

He says, "Yes my child, what can I do for you today? How can I help you? Where would you like to go today? What would you like to do? Can we go to the park together? Maybe chase butterflies together? Maybe spend some time together? What would you like me to do for you?"

"Call unto me!" God wishes that you as His child would call on Him. He wants to answer you. He desires intimate relationship with you!

Yes, He is God, Creator of the Universe and Maker of all things. Yes, He made you and He knows you. He knows when you go out and when you come in, when you go to bed and sleep, and when you are awake. Nothing is hidden from Him.

This Great Almighty God is your Father. He is your

Daddy. He desires that you call and He wants you to ask. He is waiting, He is listening, and His ears are open to your call.

Open dialogue between you and God continually develops relationship between you and Him. You will begin to really be acquainted with Him as your Father. And it will not be that you *think* you know Him, but that you *do* know Him.

You will discern when He speaks to you and you will know how He operates. You will see and recognize His hands moving in situations for you every day. You will hear His voice in the raindrops.

When you are standing at a street corner and do not understand why, you realize that He has you there for a reason. Your heart trusts in Him.

When His hands move in your life you will know that it is He and not the enemy. You will recognize that it is He when He says to you, "turn left at the next corner," or "turn right. Go here or go there, do this or do that."

> Hosea 4: 1 & 6, "Hear the word of the Lord, ye children of Israel: for the Lord hath a controversy with the inhabitants of the Land, because there is no truth, no mercy, nor knowledge of God in the Land. My people are destroyed for lack of knowledge: because thou hast rejected knowledge, I will also reject thee . . ."

God's desire for intimate, loving, and lasting relationship with His children is so great that He cries out, "My people suffer, they hurt, and they are dying because they do not know Me! My children are destroyed because they do not realize who I am!"

It is the deep cry of the heart of a Father who hurts over the sufferings of His children; children who do not know Him. They do not realize that He has their best at heart, and that He desires to do them good and not bad.

It grieves God that His children are in misery and dying. And they are suffering and perishing because *they do not know Him.*

"I love you! I am your Daddy! I care about you! When will you learn of me? When will you get to know me?" The heart of God cries out for His children with deep longing.

Testimony

A friend of mine had been in a dilemma for years. He knew he was called to the ministry and he had gone through all the steps to prepare and yet even after fourteen years, he was still working at a secular job and doing ministry part time. The desire of his heart was to serve the Lord in full time ministry.

He had prayed every step of the way and each time God seemed to be saying, "wait" or "not yet."

The answer to his serving God full time seemed to be with the armed forces as a chaplain. He applied for full time chaplaincy and doors started to open.

Yet the more doors were open, the more hurdles were placed before him and what seemed like something that should be straightforward and easy took three years, just to get an interview. He was even asked to upgrade his Master's degree with out the promise of getting in to the forces.

Steve and I have been friends for many years. We are actually more like brothers than friends. So I had witnessed these struggles and hurdles and together we prayed all along the journey.

But the real breakthrough came in God's timing. God knew Steve wanted to serve full time, but he needed to learn some things along the way.

The big interview came and only two evangelical chaplains were chosen, and Steve was not one of them. The contract of his existing job was almost finished and he just didn't know if the Lord was directing him elsewhere or what he should do.

One night, during this turmoil he came over to my apartment. In addition to the work situation, he was also driving an old car which was falling apart.

Together we prayed and wept on each other's shoulders as we have done on so many occasions. We asked God to intervene in the situation, and to open a door for Him to be able to function in the area that he was called for and had prepared for.

Although he had prayed all the way along the journey, it was time to press in and persist, knowing that God would do something.

On the very next day, Steve received a phone call from the Canadian Armed Forces. An opening had been made for another chaplain. He got the job, and he is now Padre Steve Heemskerk.

That same day, a friend from his work place spoke to both him and his wife separately about the car. He said that he understood the need for them to have a good car and he felt from the Lord that he should give them $5,000 towards the purchase of a better car.

Sometimes our faith takes us to the limit, but God meets us at that very place and takes us to the next step. He really wants us to rely on Him and not on our own strength, even when we're asking for something honorable, like a place to serve Him.

Do you believe that God cares about all of your needs, and that He wants to meet them? Sure, He does!

Another friend of mine Fred Frits Bax and his wife Janice live in Attica, Michigan. I have often spent time at their house refreshing from my trips abroad. Fred said to me once, "David, whenever you have a need, make it known."

That is something I have learned to practice with

good results. Make your needs known, and you will not regret that you did.

Relationship, Not Religious Customs

There was a time when Israel turned to idols and worshipped devils instead of God. They had forgotten their God. They did not know Him. They could not recognize His voice. They could not make out His ways and they did not have relationship with Him. They had forgotten their Father.

God's cry is that we do not do the same. God's desire is that you have knowledge of Him.

Knowing Him comes from relating to Him on a daily basis. It comes from praying and fasting, and studying His word each day. It comes from fellowship: spending time in church, with God and His children. It comes from worshipping Him.

When a child reaches a certain age, he goes to school and is trained. He reads a book, gains knowledge from it and practices that intelligence. He starts to learn and increase. He becomes skilled at new things as life brings them to him. He will fall, but he will get up and hopefully learn from his mistakes.

When he gets into trouble he turns to his father and mother for help. They have helped in the past and he realizes that they will help him again. He goes on to maturity.

He goes on to know his mother and father in greater measure and to love and respect them more and more. *This is because he has relationship with them.*

Life Begins at Birth

A child does not remain a child, but grows up. A baby must depend totally on its' parents to be fed, washed, clothed, loved, disciplined, taught, nurtured and trained up. So too must a man or woman, boy or girl, who receives new birth in Christ. They must be washed, clothed, fed, loved, disciplined, taught, nurtured and trained.

Life in God and knowledge of God begins at our new birth.

> Hosea 6: 1- 3, 6, "Come and let us return unto the Lord: for he hath torn and he will heal us; he hath smitten, and he will bind us up. After two days will he revive us: in the third day he will raise us up, and we shall live in his sight. *Then shall we know*, if we follow on to know the Lord: his going forth is prepared as the morning; and he shall come unto us as the rain, as the latter and former rain unto the earth. For I desired mercy, and not sacrifice; and the knowledge of God more than burnt offerings."

Proverbs 1: 7, "The fear of the Lord is the beginning of

knowledge."

Look at what the Lord says about you in Isaiah 49:15, "Can a woman forget her sucking child, that she should not have compassion on the son of her womb? yea, they may forget, yet *will I not forget thee.*"

Do you see the love of your Heavenly Father in these verses? Don't you see that His love exceeds that of mankind? If your mother and father forsake you, He will not. Why? God is your Father that is why!

King David also understood this truth and summed it up this way in Psalms 27: 10, "When my father and my mother forsake me, then the Lord will take me up."

The Father's love for you and I is so great. It is deep, rich, and abounding. Do you remember the great declaration and demonstration of His love on the cross when Jesus was crucified and died for you?

He held nothing back. He gave it all. He gave the best. He gave His only begotten Son. He paid the highest price. He is your Father. The Judge of all judges is your Father.

Remember, God is not looking for servants or slaves; He is seeking sons and daughters!

God waits for you with open arms. He waits for you to recognize Him and acknowledge Him as Father. He waits for you like a child who waits for his Christmas present.

Months before Christmas arrives, that child counts

every day that goes by one by one. When Christmas arrives and he has his present in his hands, he rips the wrapping off as fast as his little fingers can maneuver. His eyes light up and a great big smile appears on his face as he holds the gift in his hands. Then away he goes to enjoy his new treasure.

God Delights in You

God does not want to be out there somewhere in the distance away from you. He desires to be right here with you. He wants you to understand that He will never leave you nor forsake you.

He loves you with an everlasting love. His love for you is unending. You cannot outrun His love, you cannot hide from His love, and you cannot out give His love.

When you recognize Him as Father, approach and relate to Him as such. Every day, more and more, you will find yourself in His arms.

You will find yourself sitting at His feet listening to every word He speaks. Sometimes sitting on His knees as He wraps his loving arms tenderly around you and tells you how much He loves you. Now and again walking hand in hand with Him along a garden path; sometimes sitting on a rock overlooking the shimmering lake, or lying under a tree. You listen as He describes Heaven and tells you what He has waiting there for you.

You find that every day, little by little, more and more, you are falling more in love with your Father. You are beginning to know Him. You are beginning to see Him for who He really is. You are starting to recognize the tender hearted, loving, gentle, kind, compassionate, merciful and gracious Father that He is.

There is nowhere that you do not see Him. There isn't anywhere that you do not sense His presence. You find that He is always with you and truly never forsakes you. He is everywhere.

You feel the touch of His hand on your shoulder in the supermarket. He lets you know He is there. He talks with you in the car, in the bus, at the computer, and while you are studying. He speaks to you in dreams and in visions.

He speaks gently to you when you are walking along the street, while you are working and when you are with friends or family. He is with you always - He is your Father.

Can you feel His loving arms around you right now?

Chapter 3

COVENANTED LOVE

Tall green grass sways in the cool breeze around them. Birds sing love songs to each other from trees nearby. Bees drink nectar from delicious flowers, and tiny mammals burrow in holes under their feet. None are aware of the historical moment about to transpire amidst their humble existence.

David was still a very young man chosen and anointed by God to be the King of Israel. Jonathan was perhaps already married, and working on raising a family. They were friends, and loved each other as brothers.

Saul, the father of Jonathan and King of Israel, full of jealousy and hate, came between them. He knew that David would be the next King of Israel and was determined that this would not happen.

He wanted Jonathan to be King instead, and so he

set out to destroy David. Saul was willing to defy God even though he knew that it was God's choice that David be king. However, Jonathan confided in David and told him of his father's plan. He also spoke kindly to his father on David's behalf.

David was again safe in Saul's presence for a time. But, Saul's plans to kill David surfaced again and he once more sought to kill him. Jonathan didn't know about this, and so David told him.

They wept bitterly as they held each other. They had to say goodbye and knew not when or if they would see each other again. Their lives had been tightly woven together these last few years, but they were being torn apart by a raging mad father.

It was a painful and a somber moment. Both hearts were broken.

Neither of them had imagined this to happen; yet today it was all cascading down on them. Today they were saying goodbye, and realized that it might be the last.

Before they separated, they renewed their covenant with each other.

"Never forget me dear Jonathan."

"I will never forget you David. Not you, nor your descendants." Tears stream down his face as he grips David by the shoulders.

"We made a covenant Jonathan. Remember our

covenant. What is mine is yours. Your enemies are mine. If you ever lack, I will supply your needs. I will be your brother forever. I will fight by your side when that day comes. And if I have to, I will die for you." Sobbing uncontrollably, David held Jonathan by the arms.

They both wept and prayed together.

"May the Lord our God bless you David. May you never lack any good thing and may He subdue your enemies before you. May He lavish you with goodness that your barns be filled to overflowing, and your life be bountiful with joy."

"And may He do the same for you also Jonathan, and more."

They took their last embrace with broken hearts and turned away from each other. One last look from the distance, one last wave goodbye - they separated.

1 Samuel chapter 19 and 20

Communion

Christians all over the world partake of communion. Most partake on the first Sunday of each month, while others participate every Sunday. When sharing in communion they divide bread and wine or grape juice amongst them.

Many Christians partake of communion time after time and walk away not knowing what they have really done.

What is communion? Why do we have communion? Is there a benefit in taking communion?

The wine or grape juice represents the blood of Jesus in communion. The bread represents His broken body. Communion is also referred to as The Last Supper. This is because Jesus and His disciples shared communion the night before He died. The word communion also means spiritual union.

> Luke 22:17–20, "And He took the cup, and gave thanks, and said, Take this, and divide it among yourselves: For I say unto you, I will not drink of the fruit of the vine, until the kingdom of God shall come. And He took bread, and gave thanks, and brake it, and gave unto them, saying, This is my body which is given for you: this do in remembrance of me. Likewise also the cup after supper, saying, This cup is the *new testament* (New Covenant) in my blood, which is shed for you."

Communion is sharing in and remembering the New Testament or "The New Covenant." It is not just remembering that Jesus died for us, but that He made a covenant with us. His body was broken and His blood was shed. There is purpose behind His actions. There is deep meaning in what He did.

Jesus longed for this night with deep longing. His

mission and purpose for coming to the earth was about to be fulfilled. Nothing would be more gratifying than to accomplish His assignment. He was pleased that it was about to be completed.

"This cup is the New Testament (New Covenant)," He said.

To understand this New Covenant, we must first look at the one God made with Abraham. The representation of the contract that God made with us through Jesus is in this one.

What does this covenant mean to us? What benefits does it have for us?

> "And he brought him forth abroad, and said, Look now toward heaven, and tell the stars, if thou be able to number them: and he said unto him, So shall *thy seed* be. And he believed in the Lord; and he counted it to him for righteousness."

> "And he said unto him, Take me an heifer of three years old, and a she goat of three years old, and a ram of three years old, and a turtle dove, and a young pigeon. And he took unto him all these, and divided them in the midst, and laid each piece one against another; but the birds divided he not. And when the fowls came down upon the carcasses, Abram drove them away."

> "And it came to pass, that when the sun went down, and it was dark, behold a smoking furnace, and a burning lamp that passed between those pieces. In the same day the Lord made a *covenant* with Abram . . ."
> Genesis 15:5, 6, 9–11, 17, 18,

Covenant in the day and age of (Abram) Abraham was a lifetime binding agreement between two people or two families. It was an agreement that one must complete with his life if it was required, and often that was the case.

In this life binding contract, two people will cut the covenant or make the covenant. When doing so, the two individuals representing each other or in most cases whole families, will cut their wrists or the palm of their hands. They then clasp their hands together and allow blood to mingle.

Thereafter they pronounce *the blessing* or words of agreement of the covenant to each other. This is similar to what we saw David and Jonathan do.

Subsequently they exchanged names with each other. It is comparable to what is done in marriage. The bride takes on her husband's name after they are married.

The two people entering into the agreement would then sit down and share a covenant meal. *"You are eating my body,"* they would say. A piece of bread would then be placed in the covenant partner's mouth. *"You are drinking my blood,"* they would declare as they shared wine.

Heathens often allowed drops of their own blood to

fall into the cup of wine, and then gave the glass to the covenant partner to drink from. In making this life binding agreement they exchanged identities.

Covenant only God could Fulfill

God covenanted with Abraham and made a promise that only He could complete. He pledged to do something that was never done before by any human; something that couldn't be done by anyone else, and will never be redone.

In making this binding agreement with Abraham, God made an oath in His own name. And because there was no way that Abraham could fulfill any part of the covenant on his own, *God covenanted with Himself* to fulfill the promise.

"For when God made promise to Abraham, because he could swear by no greater, *he sware by himself* . . ."

Hebrews 6:13

> "And I will bring you in unto the land, concerning the which I did swear to give it to Abraham, to Isaac, and to Jacob; and I will give it you for an heritage: I am the lord." Exodus 6:8

Making The Covenant

Abraham divided the animals into two halves. This was the

shedding of blood by cutting. Blood must be shed in order to make the covenant.

What is so important about the shedding of blood? The Bible tells us that the life is in the blood.

> "For it is the life of all flesh; the blood of it is for the life thereof: therefore I said unto the children of Israel, Ye shall eat the blood of no manner of flesh: *for the life of all flesh is the blood* thereof: whosoever eateth it shall be cut off." Leviticus 17:14

Two figures walked in the middle of the divided carcasses as Abraham looked on. And neither of those two figures was Abraham.

The sacrifices were there in front of him having been divided into two parts and lying side by side. There was definitely blood all over them. And two figures walked in the middle of the divided pieces, mingling blood with their feet as they went, but Abraham was not one of them. Yet the covenant was being made with him.

You will remember that when two people made covenant, they would cut their hands or wrists, grip each other by the hands, and allow their blood to mingle. This signified that they were now one and it bound their agreement.

Why wasn't Abraham walking in the midst of the divided animals? Wasn't He part of the covenant? God was covenanting with him! Why didn't the Lord ask Abraham to walk in the midst of the divided carcasses?

God was making a covenant with Abraham that Abraham couldn't keep.

It was not possible for Abraham to accomplish the requirements of the covenant, and God knew this. So, He made a binding agreement with Himself with the knowledge that He alone was able to fulfill the requirements of the contract.

Abraham beheld the making of the covenant and shared in the making of it through a representative.

The two figures were a burning lamp and a smoking furnace; what were they?

The smoking furnace is the presence of the Lord God:

> "And the mount Sinai was altogether on a smoke, because *the Lord descended* upon it in fire: and the smoke thereof ascended as *smoke of a furnace* . . ." Exodus 19: 18:

> "And the lord said unto Moses, Lo, I come unto thee in a *thick cloud*, that the people may hear when I speak with thee, and believe thee for ever. And Moses told the words of the people unto the lord."
>
> Exodus 19: 9

> "And the people stood afar off, and Moses drew near unto the *thick darkness where God as*." Exodus 20:21

> "And the temple was filled with *smoke* from the glory of God, and from his power . . ."
>
> Revelation 15:8

The burning lamp is Jesus. We see this in the verses of scripture below.

> "In the beginning was the *Word,* and the Word was with God, and the *Word was God.* And the Word was made flesh, and dwelt among us . . ." John 1: 1, 4, 6, 7, 14.
>
> "Thy *word is a lamp* unto my feet, and *a light* unto my path." Psalm 119: 105,
>
> "For Zion's sake will I not hold my peace, and for Jerusalem's sake I will not rest, until the righteousness thereof go forth as brightness, and the salvation thereof as a *lamp that burneth.*" Isaiah 62: 1

Two individuals representing themselves, and in most cases whole families, will make the covenant.

Jesus representing His forefather Abraham of the flesh covenanted with Father God who represented the Godhead; the Trinity.

Jesus is the seed of Abraham in the flesh . . . Genesis, Romans, Hebrews.

> "For verily he took not on him the nature of angels; but he took on him (Christ) *the seed of Abraham.*" Hebrews 2:16

"Now to Abraham and *his seed* were the promises made. He saith not, And to seeds, as of many; but as of one, *And to thy seed, which is Christ.*" Galatians 3:16

Thousands of years before Jesus was crucified to pay the sin debt for us, He represented His earthly forefather Abraham, and covenanted with His Heavenly Father, God. Years before He came on the earth in the flesh to die, Jesus walked between bloody carcasses, and made a binding agreement that only He could accomplish by the power of Holy Spirit.

Abraham could not make such a covenant, but his seed (Jesus Christ) could. This is why the Lord did not ask Abraham to walk in the midst of the carcasses. Abraham's relationship with God was such that God shared much with him, and I am sure that He shared this truth with him also.

They covenanted that Jesus was going to die for the sins of the world and set captives free. Abraham couldn't die for the sins of the world.

"My covenant will I not break, nor alter the thing that is gone out of my lips." Psalm 89: 34

Jesus' Covenant

On the night He was betrayed, Jesus broke bread, saying, *"Eat, this is My body broken for you."*

Then He took wine and gave it to His disciples

saying, *"Drink, this is the New Testament (new covenant) in My blood."*

Before going to the cross, Jesus was beaten with whips that dug deep into His flesh. The whips used were made of braided cords with pieces of bone and, or metal, which tore His flesh from His body. He was unrecognizable after His sufferings. His body was broken and was left bleeding.

He was then taken to Golgotha where they crucified Him, piercing His hands and His feet with nails. The nails pierced the area of the hand that would have been cut in making a covenant. Blood was shed.

"Consider the cost, Beloved. Consider what it was worth to Jesus Christ to be in covenant relationship with you . . . to give you direct and unlimited access to the Father. Be still before Him." (Kay Arthur - her book, *When you need a friend There's a Covenant.*)

People making life binding agreement in those days would place a piece of bread in the other's mouth and say, "you are eating my body." Jesus broke bread and said to His disciples, *"This is my body broken for you."*

And then they were given the cup of wine and told,

"You are drinking my blood."

Our Lord covenanted with the disciples on that special night. Thus, every time that you share in communion, you remember Jesus and what He did for you. But, you also *renew the covenant* He made with you on the cross.

You will remember that when two people made a covenant they exchanged identities.

> "And He took the cup, and gave thanks, and said, take this, and divide it among yourselves: For I say unto you, I will not drink of the fruit of the vine, until the kingdom of
>
> God shall come. And He took bread, and gave thanks, and brake it, and gave unto them, saying, this is my body which is given for you: this do in remembrance of me. Likewise also the cup after supper, saying, this cup is the *new testament* (New Covenant) in my blood, which is shed for you."
>
> Luke 22:17–20

After that night Jesus went to the cross, taking your sin, shame, guilt and your debt with Him. He exchanged His life for yours. He died, He was buried, and He rose again. He became a curse for you.

> "Christ hath redeemed us from the curse of the law, being made a curse for us: for it is written, Cursed is every one that hangeth on a tree (cross) . . ." Galatians 3:13, 14

God told Abraham (who was called Abram at the time) what He was covenanting to do for Him. He was going to make him, "Father of many nations." He was going to give him a land to dwell in and He was going to give him *a son*, and through this son, all nations of the earth would be blessed.

He then gave him a new name, Abraham, which means father of many nations.

> "And if ye be Christ's, then are ye *Abraham's seed*, and heirs according to the promise."
>
> Galatians 3:29

> "And they sung a new song, saying, Thou art worthy to take the book, and to open the seals thereof: for Thou wast slain, and hast *redeemed us to God* by thy blood out of every kindred, and tongue, and people, and *nation*; And hast made us unto our God kings and priests: and we shall reign on the earth."
>
> Revelation 5: 9

Switching Places

In covenant with God through Christ Jesus we have been given a new name, and a new identity; Christian. By taking on Christ's name in covenant we also take on His identity and all that is His becomes ours.

> "The Spirit itself beareth witness with our spirit, that we are children of God: And if children heirs; heirs of God, and joint *heirs*

> *with Christ . . .*" Romans 8:16, 17
>
> "Christ hath redeemed us from the curse of the law, being made a curse for us: for it is written, Cursed is every one that hangeth on a tree: *That the blessing of Abraham might come on the gentiles, through Jesus Christ*; that we might receive the promise of the Spirit through faith. Now to Abraham and his seed were the promises made. He saith not, And to seeds, as of many; but as of one, And to thy seed, which is Christ."
>
> Galatians 3:13, 14, 16

When Christ went to the cross, He took my old identity; my sinful nature, and nailed it to the cross.

He then gave me a new identity: His life, His power, His nature, His righteousness, His Godliness, His kingdom, His wealth, His peace, His joy, His strength, His perfection and all that is His.

> "My covenant will I not break, nor alter the thing that is gone out of my lips."
>
> Psalm 89: 34,
>
> "And Jesus came and spake unto them, saying, All power is given unto me in heaven and earth." Matthew 28:16,
>
> "Behold, I give unto you power to tread on serpents and scorpions, and over all the

> power of the enemy: and nothing shall by any means hurt you." Luke 10:19

All of this now belongs to you because *you have taken on His name and identity.*

> "But put ye on the Lord Jesus Christ, and make not provision for the flesh, to fulfil the lusts thereof." Romans 13:14

> "And that ye put on *the new man*, which after God is *created in righteousness and true holiness.*" Ephesians 4:24

> "And have put on the new man, which *is renewed after the image of him that created him.*" Colossians 3:10

And since you have exchanged life with Christ and taken on His identity, *all* that is His is yours. And *all* that is yours is His. He left every sin and all manner of evil that pertain to you and yours on the cross.

> "Know ye not, that so many of us as were baptized into Jesus Christ were baptized into His death? Therefore we are buried with him by baptism into his death: that *like as Christ was raised up* from the dead by the glory of the Father, *even so we also should walk in newness of life.* For if we have been planted together in the likeness of his death, we shall be also in the likeness of his resurrection:" Romans 6: 3–5

Since Christ took your sinful nature, your sickness and weaknesses, failures, doubts and fears *and all that you were* to the cross, it means that when He died, you died.

> "Knowing this, *that our old man is crucified with him*, that the body of sin might be destroyed, that henceforth we should not serve sin. For he that is dead is freed from sin. Now if we be dead with Christ, we believe that we shall also live with him: Likewise reckon ye yourselves dead indeed unto sin, but alive unto God through Jesus Christ our Lord." Romans 6: 6–8, 11

> "*I am crucified with Christ*: nevertheless I live; yet not I, but *Christ liveth in me*: and the life which I now live in the flesh I live by the faith of the Son of God, who loved me, and gave himself for me." Galatians 2: 20,

Jesus took to the cross your nature, your sin, your faults, your failures, your shame, your difficulties, your weaknesses, your imperfections, your ungodliness, your poverty, your sorrows, your pain, and your sickness. He took everything that was the *old you* and nailed all of it to the cross. And that is where *you* must remain - on the cross - crucified. For if *you live* Christ cannot live in and through you. You must die. And you did die! *You were crucified with Christ.*

> "And when he had called the people unto him with his disciples also, he said unto them, Whosoever will come after me, let him deny

> himself, and take up his cross, and follow me. For whosoever will save his life shall lose it; but whosoever shall lose his life for my sake and the gospel's, the same shall save it." Mark 8: 34, 35

Therefore you deny yourself. But, what is the significance of denying self? It simply means that you refuse to live for you. You decline to satisfy your own cravings and selfish desires.

It is no longer you who live, but Christ who lives in you.

"For to me to live is Christ, and to die is gain." Philippians 1:21

So you deny yourself of life in the flesh. You deny yourself life in the world and its sinful pleasures. You are dead. You died on the cross with Christ.

Jesus said, *"Take up your cross and follow me."* What does that imply?

It means that while you are on this earth, always see yourself as dead. It is not you who govern any longer, but Christ. It is not you who rule any longer, but Christ in you. See yourself this way; not as the one who walks, runs, eats, sleeps, thinks, speaks and acts, but Christ who does them in and through you.

"For it is God which worketh in you both to will and to do of his good pleasure." Philippians 2:13

That is what it means to take up your cross and

follow Christ. It doesn't mean that you are to punish yourself, or take up suffering and pain as a form of carrying your cross. That is not what it means! It simply implies that you see yourself as dead.

Now, if you are dead there is no shame, no pain, no disappointment, no fear of failure, and no low self-esteem, etc.

Act and live as if you are dead. Do not live for you any longer, but live for and unto God. And when you do the *life* of Christ will flow and be evident in you. Then you will see the great and wonderful things that God can do through you!

Jesus became a curse for you when He took on Himself your sinfulness, your sickness, your ungodliness, your shame, and all that is of your old nature. And as He hung on the cross and died, you died. He now is the portal, the doorway, and entrance into Heaven.

"Jesus saith unto him, I am the way, the truth, and the life: no man cometh unto the Father, but by me." John 14:6,

As Jesus hangs between Heaven and earth, He forms a bridge between God and mankind. You can step up to the cross, enter into Heaven through Christ as the doorway, and sit next to God your Father in Him.

"For in Him we live, and move, and have our being . . ." Acts 17:28a

"And hath raised us up together, and made us sit

together in heavenly places in Christ Jesus." Ephesians 2:6

His Riches Are Yours

So, what does it mean to take up your cross and follow Him? Like Jesus, you rose from the dead. Jesus was taken off the cross, placed in a tomb and three days later He rose from the grave.

The cross of Jesus is empty. So too is yours. You died with Christ, were taken off the cross, buried and rose again with Him. Hallelujah! Your cross is empty.

So when Jesus said, *"Deny yourself and take up your cross and follow me,"* He was saying to deny yourself of weakness, of sickness, of ungodliness, of unrighteousness, of death and hell and all that is of the devil; all that is part of the old you.

You are no longer the person you were. You are a new creation. Since you exchanged identity with Christ through covenant, *you now have His life in all its fullness.*

> "And hath put all things under his feet, and gave him to be the head over all things to the church, which is his body (*you*), the fulness of him that filleth all in all."
>
> Ephesians 1:22, 23

> "For it pleased the Father that in him should all fulness dwell;" Colossians 1:19

"For in him dwelleth all the fulness of the Godhead bodily." Colossians 2:9

He was not asking you to take up burdens, heavy loads, shame and guilt, troubles and torments, sin or sickness. No! Jesus has called us into rest, not into carrying heavy burdens.

"For my yoke is easy, and my burden is light." Matthew 11:30

Take up your cross and follow Him. Let everyone know that you died. Show to the world that you no longer live, but Christ lives in you. Take up resurrection life and follow Jesus! Fill up with His power which is already in you and join Him. Put on love and emulate Him. This is the covenant of love that Christ made with you!

Chapter 4

EFFICACY OF LOVE

"To know love is to surrender to love."

With its green grass, lush trees, gurgling brook and seclusion, it provided the tranquility and quiet solitude for resting and meditating. It is a place that they have often resorted to after a long day. It is a place of refuge and serenity.

After many hours of ministry to the multitude, it was a retreat from it all.

On bended knees He prays. A little way from Him, His disciples have fallen asleep with weariness. But, His mind is full of memories.

They were not only followers, but also His friends and His helpers. Having been with Him for about three and a half years they had become close to His heart, tenderly loved by Him.

Many times He had been there for them. He had healed Peter's mother-in-law, directed Him to catch a fish which had a gold piece in its mouth to pay taxes, and had enabled him to walk on water.

Once when the storm was raging around them in the sea, He was asleep in the boat. They had called out to him, "Master, we are going to die." He calmed the storm and rescued them.

Another time, there was a dispute between them about who would be the greatest. He assured them that it was the one who served.

He had watched them rejoice over the results after He gave them power over the enemy. And on yet another occasion, He was transfigured before Peter, James, and John.

Sorrow fills His heart as He meditates. Tears fall from His eyes mingling with the dew on the grass. He prays for their lives, their testimony, and their relationships. He prays for their protection, and He prays for their guidance.

He had shared their lives and knew them well. He was aware that they would miss Him. He recognized that they would stumble and fall from time to time and make mistakes.

They would face many hardships, and they would be hurt and suffer for the gospel. Some would even die horrible deaths. For this, He was extremely sorrowful.

Now He would no longer physically be with them. But He knew that this was how it had to be.

He turns and looks at them. From where He is, He can see some of them sleeping peacefully. They do not know what He is about to suffer at the hands of men. So they rest, being tired from a very long day. He turns back to praying.

A picture of men hanging on crosses materializes in His mind. Wounded, disfigured, bleeding and dying, they cry out in pain. He had seen the horrible deaths of others on the cross. And knowing all things, He knew what death He was about to face.

Even now He feels the pain; the nails in His hands and His feet, the crown of thorns in His head, the stripes on His back. He can feel the heat of the scorching sun burning into His wounds. He can sense the dryness in His throat as moisture and strength drain from His broken body.

He envisions Himself gasping for air as the breath leaves His body. Devoid of strength, He is unable to pull Himself up to take another gulp of air.

He can taste the bitterness of vinegar on His tongue. He hears the jeers of men, the laughter of women, and the mockery of children.

He wishes that Father would do this some other way. In agony He cries, "Take this cup from me. Not my will, but yours, be done."

His sweat drips from His body as great drops of blood.

> " . . . And He came out, and went, as He was wont, to the Mount of Olives; and His disciples also followed Him. And when He was at the place, He said unto them, 'Pray that ye enter not into temptation.'
>
> And He was withdrawn from them about a stone's cast, and kneeled down, and prayed, saying, 'Father, if Thou be willing, remove this cup from me: nevertheless not My will, but Thine, be done.' And there appeared an angel unto Him from Heaven, strengthening Him. And being in an agony He prayed more earnestly: and His sweat was as it were great drops of blood falling down to the ground." Luke 22: 39 to 44

Malchus' Story

I am standing by the gate. They lead Him through with soldiers on each side, others following.

The one who cut off my ear follows behind at a distance. He can't see me. I am standing to one side, and there are many people entering the High Priest's house.

For some unknown reason I feel no anger or

displeasure toward this man. As a matter of fact, I feel pity for him. The sad, broken-hearted look on his face is not hidden under the shadowy light of the torches. He seems very troubled.

Could it be because his Master won't let him fight back? Could it be because he feels sorry for cutting off my ear? Or, is it because he is afraid of what they might do to this Teacher? He must love Him very much because he did try to fight for Him.

They are just going to try the prisoner Jesus for mischief, maybe chastise Him and let Him go. Perhaps they will keep Him in prison for a short time until everything has cooled off.

When I caught the blow to my ear earlier, I thought for a moment that was the end for me. It had all happened so suddenly.

Grabbing the right side of my head with my hands I had dropped to my knees in pain. There was blood all over that side of my face and my hand. A loud scream had gone from my lips, and with pain surging through my head I was scared and trembling.

Then I felt someone's hand removing mine from that side of my head. Suddenly, the blood stopped and there was no more pain. He helped me up. And as I stood up, I placed my hand to my head and my ear was there! It was back on! What happened? I looked at Him. Our eyes met and held.

I have never understood love until that moment. Love more intense than I have ever felt before. Love so supreme and so great that a sinner such as I could be swept over by it, and be transformed by its power and force never before experienced. It was only a touch of His hands, a look in His eyes, and words from His lips. It was an encounter that I will never forget.

Could this man really be the Son of God? Could He really be the Christ?

The look on His face as He passes me by is one of deep focus and concentration. He looks straight past me and there is no hesitation in His steady, deliberate steps.

He seems like a man on a great, urgent mission. He seems like someone who knows where He is going and what He is about to do. Does He know what is going to happen to Him?

The crowd has now entered through the gate. I hurry along. I do not want to miss any detail. I want to see what decision they are going to make concerning Him. They might even set Him free this very night.

The one who cut off my ear is sitting by the fi re with some others. He is preoccupied and has his head bent over. I wonder what his thoughts are. I pass him hurriedly, and move closer to where the prisoner Jesus is.

As I get closer I see that they have blindfolded Him.

They are spitting out all kinds of questions at Him. Suddenly, one of the men slaps Him on the face and they all begin to laugh.

Why is this? Why are they hitting Him? This is wrong. I know it is wrong. Why are they doing these things to this man? He didn't do any harm to them.

I must get closer. I want to help, I must help, but what can I do?

I am just a servant of the High Priest. If I say anything or try to do anything, they might do the same to me. But this is terrible! This is outrageous! He is going to be tried, why don't they wait for the trial?

I was with them all along. I went with them to get Jesus. I had the same mind as they did, to bring Him to trial and to punish Him. I was in agreement with them to try Jesus as a common criminal. Now I feel only love and compassion for Him.

I could have been doing the same thing to this man as they are doing to Him now . . . if His love had not penetrated my heart the way it did!

The thought made me shudder. I detest the very idea of harming such a man, someone who has been good and kind to me.

I wanted to do evil to Him! I wanted to bring this man before a judge, and see Him punished for crimes I do not even know He committed!

Again they hit Him. And they are saying such awful things to Him! The blasphemy that is coming out of their mouths! The rotten things they are uttering! "Prophesy!" they say, "Who is it that is hitting you?"

How could any man treat another human being in such a way? How can we, being human and of higher intelligence above all created flesh, ill-treat another person the way we do? How can we?

In all of what they do to Him, He says not a word. Neither does He try to defend Himself.

As they continued their mocking and tormenting, I became more and more tired and disheartened. It was a very long day. I retreated to a pillar nearby.

It is now morning and they are taking Him into council. Sometime during all of it, I had fallen asleep right where I was sitting, beside the pillar.

> "When they which were about Him saw what would follow, they said unto Him, 'Lord, shall we smite with the sword?' And one of them smote the servant of the high priest, and cut off his right ear. And Jesus answered and said, 'Suffer ye thus far.' And He touched his ear, and healed him." Luke 22: 49 to 51
>
> "Then Simon Peter having a sword drew it, and smote the high priest's servant, and cut off his right ear. The servant's name was Malchus." John 18: 10
>
> "And when they had blindfolded Him, they struck Him on the face, and asked Him,

> saying, 'Prophesy, who is it that smote Thee?'" Luke 22:64

At the well

I could see that He was a Jew and I was not too thrilled that He was here. He was sitting on the ledge of the mouth of the well as if He was the owner.

We Samaritans do not have dealings with Jews. We do not like them and they do not like us. I wished that this Jew wasn't here. But He was, and I needed water for my house.

Trying not to catch His eyes I approached cautiously around the opposite side from where He was. I lowered the pail into the well.

"Lady . . ."

"Oh no . . ." Under my breath slipped the words.

" . . . Give me water to drink?"

"But Sir, you are a Jew. Why do you ask me for a drink? You know that we Samaritans have no dealings with you Jews."

I was hoping that He would pass on. I didn't want anyone from my village to see me with a Jewish man. What would they say if they did? I mean, they already don't have too many nice things to say about me. But, He continued,

"Lady, if you knew the gift of God and who I am,

you would ask of me and I would give you living water."

"But Sir, you do not have anything to lower into the well to get water, and how are you going to give me water to drink?" I looked away from Him with a witty smile on my face.

I really can't understand how He could give me water to drink when I am the one with the leather bucket. I do not think that He truly knows what He is talking about.

"Sir, where are you going to get this living water from? This well is deep and you do not have a leather bucket like I do.

Are you greater than our father Jacob who gave us this well? Are you by some great act or miracle going to give me this water you talk about?" I was really wondering now.

How is He going to give me water to drink? These Jews think they are so smart.

"Lady, after you drink from this well you will thirst again. But if anyone drinks the water that I give, he will *never thirst again*. It will be in him *a well of living water* which springs up into everlasting life."

He was very sincere and seemed serious. Could He really do this? Could He really give me this special water so that I do not have to come back to this well to get water? Nor will I ever thirst again? I mean, this would be the greatest thing yet! I will never have to return here in this heat for water, and I will not need to drink water ever again!

I think I will ask Him for *this water*. Maybe He has a way of getting water from the well, and by some miracle He can cause it to always satisfy my thirst.

"Sir, give me this water!"

"Go back to the village and bring your husband with you."

My husband . . . ? What does He want with my husband? The guy is not even my husband! "Sir, I do not have a husband."

"You say the truth. You have had five husbands, and the one you now have is not your husband."

What! How could He know this? How could he possibly know? This is the first time I have laid eyes on this man and He recognizes this about me? Has someone told Him, but whom? He must be a prophet . . .

"Sir, I can see that you are a prophet."

There was always an unanswered question in my mind. Let's see if He really is a prophet.

"Sir, our fathers worshiped in this mountain. You Jews worship in Jerusalem and you say that is where people ought to worship. Does this mean that we do not really worship God?"

If this is the case, the Samaritan Rabbis who are always accusing me, are themselves very wrong. They do not really worship God. I am thereby justified. They are just like me.

"You do not know whom you worship. We know whom we worship, and salvation is of the Jews. The time is coming and it is now, when true worshippers will worship Father God in spirit and in truth. This is what the Father desires."

Well, I do not know about that! Telling me I do not know whom I worship!

"Messiah is coming! He is known as Christ! And when He comes He will tell us all things!"

"I am, the Christ."

What? The Christ? I am talking to the Messiah? He is actually here, talking to me! It can't be! But…? What if…?

"Sir, please wait here. I will be back. Please wait…"

The Messiah? Here? I can't believe it. I was talking to . . . The Rabbis will know! I will ask them to come and see Him for themselves. They will be able to tell me. They should be able to tell! I must hurry.

Where could Rabbi be? Maybe he is at the Synagogue. Perhaps he is at home with his family. Oh, there he is.

"Rabbi, Rabbi!" I must catch my breath.

"Come quickly, please! There is a man at the well who says that He is the Christ. Please come and see for yourself and tell me if this is really so. He told me everything that He shouldn't know about me. He must be

Christ! He must be! Come quickly, please."

"Christ." The word spread like grass fire.

"The Messiah is here! The one they call Christ is here!"

Soon everyone had heard the news, and the crowd became larger and larger as the entire village came out to meet Him. Many of us received living water that day, and our lives were changed forever.

" . . . It will be in him a fountain of living water." John 4

> "There cometh a woman of Samaria to draw water: Jesus saith unto her, "Give me to drink." (For His disciples were gone away unto the city to buy meat.) Then saith the woman of Samaria unto Him, "How is it that thou, being a Jew, askest drink of me, which am a woman of Samaria? for the Jews have no dealings with the Samaritans."
>
> Jesus answered and said unto her, "If thou knewest the gift of God, and who it is that saith to thee, 'Give me to drink;' thou wouldest have asked of Him, and He would have given thee living water."
>
> The woman saith unto Him, "Sir, thou hast nothing to draw with, and the well is deep: from whence then hast thou that living water? Art thou greater than our father Jacob, which

gave us the well, and drank thereof himself, and his children, and his cattle?" Jesus answered and said unto her, "Whosoever drinketh of this water shall thirst again: But whosoever drinketh of the water that I shall give him shall never thirst; but the water that I shall give him shall be in him a well of water springing up into everlasting life.

The woman saith unto Him, "Sir, give me this water, that I thirst not, neither come hither to draw." Jesus saith unto her, "Go, call thy husband and come hither." The woman answered and said "I have no husband." Jesus said unto her, "Thou hast well said, 'I have no husband': For thou hast had five husbands; and he whom thou now hast is not thy husband: in that saidst thou truly."

The woman saith unto Him, "Sir, I perceive that Thou art a prophet. Our fathers worshipped in this mountain; and ye say, that in Jerusalem is the place where men ought to worship." Jesus saith unto her, "Woman, believe Me, the hour cometh, when ye shall neither in this mountain, nor yet at Jerusalem, worship the Father. Ye worship ye know not what: we know what we worship for salvation is of the Jews. But the hour cometh, and now is, when the true worshippers shall worship the Father in spirit and in truth: for the Father seeketh such to worship Him.

God is a Spirit: and they that worship Him must worship Him in spirit and in truth."

The woman saith unto Him, "I know that Messias cometh, which is called Christ: when He is come, He will tell us all things." Jesus saith unto her, "I that speak unto thee am He."

And upon this came His disciples, and marvelled that He talked with the woman: yet no man said, "What seekest thou?" or, "Why talkest thou with her?"

The woman then left her waterpot, and went her way into the city, and saith to the men, "Come, see a man, which told me all things that ever I did: is not this the Christ?"

Then they went out of the city, and came unto Him.

In the mean while His disciples prayed Him, saying "Master, eat."

But He said unto them, "I have meat to eat that ye know not of."

Therefore said the disciples one to another, "Hath any man brought Him aught to eat?"

Jesus saith unto them, "My meat is to do the will of Him that sent me, and to finish His work. Say not ye, 'There are yet four months, and then cometh harvest?' behold, I say unto you, 'Lift up your eyes, and look on the fields; for they are white already to harvest.'

And he that reapeth receiveth wages, and gathereth fruit unto life eternal: that both he that sowest and he that reapeth may rejoice together.

And herein is that saying true, 'One soweth, and another reapeth.'

I sent you to reap that whereon ye bestowed no labour; other men laboured, and ye are entered into their labours."

And many of the Samaritans of that city believed on Him for the saying of the woman, which testified, "He told me all that I ever did."

So when the Samaritans were come unto Him, they besought Him that He should tarry with them: and He abode there two days.

And many more believed because of His own word; And said unto the woman, "Now we believe, not because of thy saying: for we have heard Him ourselves, and know that this is indeed the Christ, the Saviour of the world." John 4: 7 to 42

Zacchaeus

Why God made me so short I truthfully do not know. As if there wasn't enough calcium or something for bones, and enough stretchy stuff to stretch me a little. And this barrel of a tummy that I carry with me everywhere I go, is only good for wholesome delightful food.

How I wish that I had genes like Samson; tall and handsome; chiseled chest and arms; muscles all over and legs like pillars that could hold up a mountain. But . . .

There is a great crowd coming down the street. There are too many people. I won't be able to see Him. He definitely won't be able to see me.

How am I going to get Him to see me? Hmmm, I am not sure. Ah, that tree at the side of the road. I think I might be able to climb up a ways so that I can see Him. Maybe then, He will see me too.

What could He look like anyway? Ordinary? Maybe He is tall and handsome? Maybe He is muscular and strong? Do you think, maybe, He is short like me? Hmmm, I wonder?

Uh, ah, it's not easy climbing this tree, especially at this age, with these short arms and legs. But . . . uh, ah . . . I am here. I'll just sit right here and wait.

There is a lot of noise, a lot of commotion, pushing and pressing. It seems that everyone wants to touch Him. Everyone wants to get close to Him. People from the outside of the crowd try to push their way to Him.

However, there are a number of men it seems who are with Him, and who try to keep the people away. Sometimes someone does actually make it to Him.

I think I see Him . . . over there . . . I am not sure . . . Yes . . . yes, that must be Him. He is in the middle of the crowd. Some of the people have already passed by right under me. Oh boy, am I ever going to get a bird's eye view of Him!

"Zacchaeus!"

Who is calling me? It seems to come from below.

"Zacchaeus!"

It's Him! He is right under my tree, and He is calling my name!

"Come down Zacchaeus. I am going to your house today."

"You are going to my house?"

"Yes Zacchaeus, come down."

He is going to my house? My house! Oh boy! Wait till my friends hear about this. My family, what are they going to say? But, my house, why?

I am not such a good guy like some guys that I know. I am a rich man yes, but I do not frequent the synagogue as often as I ought to, and I do not give to God as I should.

When I collect taxes for the government, perhaps I bend a little, and some of it stays with me. Maybe, I take a little more from the people than I should.

So much has been said about this man. So much talk of healings and deliverances. They say He has even raised the dead. How can one man do so much good? What an interesting fellow.

"Sir . . . here is my house. Please, come in. Sit here, and make yourself welcome. Who are these others coming in behind us? Sir, are these people with you?"

"Yes Zacchaeus, they are with me."

One, two, three . . . Uh, there are twelve, and they look hungry too. I had better get the cook.

"Lord, half of all that I have I will give to the poor. And if I took anything from any man falsely, I will give back four times what was taken."

"Zacchaeus, today salvation has come to your house."

> "And Jesus entered and passed through Jericho. And behold, there was a man named Zacchaeus, which was the chief among the publicans, and he was rich. And he sought to see Jesus who He was; and could not for the press, because he was little of stature. And he ran before, and climbed up into a sycamore tree to see Him: for He was to pass that way. And when Jesus came to the place He looked up and saw Him, and said unto him, "Zacchaeus, make haste and come

down; for today I must abide at your house." And he made haste, and came down, and received Him joyfully.

And when they saw it, they all murmured, saying, that he was gone to be guest with a man that is a sinner. And Zacchaeus stood, and said unto the Lord; "Behold, Lord, the half of my goods I give to the poor; and if I have taken any thing from any man by false accusation, I restore him fourfold." And Jesus said unto him, "This day is salvation come to this house, forsomuch as he also is a son of Abraham. For the Son of man is come to seek and to save that which was lost."

Luke 19: 1 to 10

Touched by the Master's Hands

As he pulled me to my feet, it felt like thousands of fingers tickling me at the same time, like many needles prickling me from the waist down. Before I realized it, I was leaping into the air. I was on my feet!

For the first time in my life I am standing on my feet! I am upright! I am walking! I am healed!

When I reached out my hands to these men I was hoping for a little change; some money to buy some food, something to help out at home. I was not expecting what I received!

I am not sure what words came out of my mouth. I am not certain what sound I made. But the sharpness and excitement in my voice gathered the people. They came running toward us from everywhere. I was still holding on to his hands as the crowd came together.

A regular stroll turned into another exciting and memorable episode on a grand scale. Two friends, companions, disciples of Jesus, walked together to the temple. It was Peter and John, and it was the hour of prayer.

They were recently baptized in the Holy Ghost and speaking in tongues. With a fi re burning on the inside of them, their lives were never to be the same again. There was courage and an overwhelming force within them, and a passion that consumes the soul.

Once fishermen by trade, now touched by the Master's hand they were going fishing for souls.

Having been taught the value of the souls of men, there presently was an incredible desire inside them to see people change. Peter and John were consumed by a powerful love for others.

Lives were what mattered now. Lives of people in bondage; held in the grips of an enemy they did not recognize, and on their way to hell.

The love that engulfed them was not the kind that one usually feels for people. It was not a simple love; it was the love of God. *It was God.*

It was beautiful, and that was its name. At this gate waited a crippled man - me, begging for whatever I might receive to sustain my life. The appointed day had arrived, but no one knew it.

Walking to the temple was an everyday thing. They must have passed by me every time since frequenting the temple. But never before were they moved to do anything like this. Now it was different. This time it was not only a moving to do, but also more of an act that had to be done.

I was at the temple's door begging for anything that would be given to me. I had no idea that the hand that was going to receive mine was going to change my life forever.

The thought never entered my mind that the same power of the Master's hand that had touched Peter's life, was going to touch mine.

I stretched out my hand to Peter. I reached out asking for help. What I received was not what I was looking for. It was exactly what I needed.

Peter looked me straight in the eyes, clutched my hands in his and said, "Silver and Gold I do not have, but what I have, I give to you!"

Well, my friend, there certainly isn't anything in your hand that I can see, but if you have anything good to give me, I'll take it!

"Rise up and walk!" exclaimed Peter, as He pulled

me up.

Immediately, a surge of power overwhelmed me, and an amazing force flowed through me that caused me to jump to my feet. And leaping and dancing I praised God.

"Hey! I am healed! I am healed! Look at me! I am completely healed! Aha, look closer, it's me! I'm the one who used to beg at the corner, remember? Look at me, I am healed, I am healed. Look at my feet, my legs, and my body. Look here! I am healed! Ha, ha, ha, ha, ha . . ."

The crowds came running together. They surrounded me.

"Why, what happened? What has happened to him?" they called out to one another in awe. Others were laughing and dancing with me in excitement.

The sound of "He is healed, He is healed" resonated all around. "He is really healed," could be heard amidst the sound of running feet of those who were gathering. Soon the word arrived at my home.

"Your son is healed! Your brother is healed!"

Gathering skirt tails together they came running. Throwing on a shirt they dashed to the scene. Pulling on a slipper, they ran to see what all the excitement was about. Everyone wanted to know. Everyone wanted to see.

"I am healed, touched by the Master's hands."

> "Now Peter and John went up together into the temple at the hour of prayer, being the

ninth hour. And a certain man lame from his mother's womb, was carried, whom they laid daily at the gate of the temple which is called Beautiful, to ask alms of them that entered into the temple;

Who seeing Peter and John about to go into the temple asked an alms. And Peter, fastening his eyes upon him with John, said, "Silver and gold have I none; but such as I have give I thee: In the name of Jesus Christ of Nazareth rise up and walk."

And he took him by the right hand, and lifted him up: and immediately his feet and ankle bones received strength.

And he leaping up stood, and walked, and entered with them into the temple, walking, and leaping, and praising God. And all the people saw him walking and praising God: and they knew that it was he which sat for alms at the Beautiful gate of the temple: and they were filled with wonder and amazement at that which had happened unto him.

And as the lame man which was healed held Peter and John, all the people ran together unto them in the porch that is called Solomon's, greatly wondering." Acts 3: 1–11

Chapter 5

LOVE UNBOUNDED

"Surrender your all to Him and you will receive all of Him"

God loves you with an everlasting love. As a matter of fact *He loves you as much as He loves Himself.* If He didn't love you as much as He loves Himself, He wouldn't have said to you to love your neighbor as much as you love yourself. God is love. And He can do nothing, but love.

He loves you so much that He sent Jesus to die on the cross two thousand years ago. God stood back and watched His Son beaten, spat upon, scorned, despised, ridiculed, and rejected. The very ones that He loved so dearly, the very people that he created, the same ones that He sent Jesus to die for, beat Him, and forced Him to carry His own cross.

God stood back and watched them nail Jesus to a cross. He stood back and watched them raise and drop that cross into the ground. He beheld the Son He had sent; His only begotten, suffering and dying for you and for me.

There was your Father; God, caught between the love that He has for you, and the love that He has for His only begotten son.

It kept Him from taking Jesus off the cross, holding Him in His arms, loving Him and saying, "I won't go through with it. I can't go through with it. It hurts too much to see Him suffer."

It was love that kept Him from doing just that! It was everything that is God. God is love! And because He loves you, He causes all things to work out for your good.

All Things Work Out For Good

"And we know that all things work together for good to those who love God, to those who are called according to His purpose." Romans 8:28

Ney Esser is President of Agua Viva - Living Water; a ministry to the poor which I founded in 2004. He is a wonderful brother in the Lord and an encouragement to me. Ney and I went to visit a family one Monday night in Uberlândia. I had business to conduct with them. It was my first time meeting the husband, and he was a little hesitant to come out and meet us. I quickly found out why.

The left side of his face was badly cut from the forehead above the left eye to somewhere below his ears.

He had gone to the hospital and had received about eight stitches to the wound. He also lost three teeth and bruised his hand and elbow.

He had been in an accident which was the second in the last three months.

I can tell you, he was not looking too good! It was a bad accident and he could have been killed.

Just by looking at him you would not believe that he had simply fallen off his bicycle. And it was the second time that it had happened. Falling, he crashed into the curb doing damage to his body. The last time, it was the other side of his face that was injured.

Hearing all of this, I knew that he needed Jesus. I began to ask some pointed questions.

I found out that a Christian man had visited him that very morning and had prayed with him weeping. But he didn't receive Jesus Christ as Lord and Savior.

Knowing that he needed Jesus, and suspecting that the enemy was trying to get him out of the way, I persisted in sharing with him. I told him exactly what I shared with another young man at church the night before.

I made him understand that he didn't have to clean himself up and make himself ready for God. God accepts him just the way he is. I explained that he only needed to accept Jesus Christ as Lord and Savior, and then allow Jesus to clean him up from the inside.

"Jesus didn't come for perfect people. He came to make imperfect people perfect."

After clarifying some more things with him, he received Jesus Christ as his Lord and Savior. He later asked me for my number. And he also wanted to know that if he had any problems, if it was possible to phone me at any time. "Of course," I told him, "any time of the day."

God allowed these two accidents, and this man came to recognize his need for salvation.

And because of this "*bad*" he was able to come to the place of receiving salvation. God did not *make* him fall off his bicycle, but He *allowed* it to happen for the man's good.

"In every thing give thanks: for this is the will of God in Christ Jesus concerning you." Thessalonians 5:18

If God allows everything, then you need to be thankful. Instead of complaining, you need to thank Him for all things, both bad and good. If it is bad, it is once again His love in action, allowing bad that you might have good.

Death on the Cross

Death on a cross is a bad thing. It is a horrible thing. Yet God allowed it for our good.

The greatest act of God was standing aside and watching men brutalize His Son, torture Him, nail Him to a cross and leave Him hanging there until He died.

Wouldn't you say that was the utmost act of love? Wouldn't you say that was the most unselfish thing you have ever seen or heard of being done for anyone?

This He did, causing *all things* to work together for your good.

God permitted His Son to suffer pain, ridicule, and rejection for you. He allowed Him to carry your sins, and the sins of the whole world upon Himself to the cross.

God allows everything to work out for good. He permits both good and bad things to happen, and causes them to work out for your good.

Ephesians 5:20 "Giving thanks *always* for *all* things unto God and the Father in the name of our Lord Jesus Christ,"

It is not only for good things that we give God thanks, but also for bad things. We give thanks for *all things* because God causes all things to work out for good. We do not understand how He does it, but He does it.

Romans 8:28 "All things work together for good, for those who love God and are called to His purpose."

We observe an alcoholic deep in his addiction, drunk, and appearing to be out of his mind. He beats up his wife and children, and we do not want to or choose to give thanks for him, do we? He is a menace to society, a pain to his family and destruction to his own self.

A drug addict is likely to do the same thing. To satisfy his addiction, he might go to the length of stealing, prostituting, breaking and entering, or robbing someone on the street to satisfy his cravings.

Then there is the drug dealer, the thief, the drunk driver who kills or maims someone on the street. The rapist, the murderer . . . the list goes on. We do not choose to give thanks for these people or for the crimes which they commit, do we?

The Bible says to *give thanks for all things*. That is, for both bad things and for good things. When we give thanks to God for all things, what are we doing? We are recognizing that He is Sovereign and that He is in control of everything.

There is absolutely nothing that the devil would like to do, that he can just go ahead and do. He cannot do anything unless God allows him.

Look at the story of Job. Satan came to God and asked Him permission to do harm to Job. He couldn't have just gone ahead and done it. God, knowing Job's heart and knowing what He would Himself do for Job at the end of it all, gave the devil permission. He knew the end of Job's story, just as He knows the end of every story.

Joseph is another example. God revealed to Joseph in a dream that he would be a great ruler one day. Joseph's brothers were not happy about the dream he had, neither was his father and mother. His parents loved him very much, but his brothers were jealous of him.

There was a time when Jacob sent Joseph to a place where his brothers were tending the flocks. He was wearing his beautiful, multi colored coat which his father had made for him.

Joseph's brothers feared he would be ruler over them one day, and were very jealous of him. They ripped his multi colored coat off him and threw him into a pit. Later they took him out and sold him to men traveling to Egypt.

In Egypt, Joseph was falsely accused and placed in prison. Forgotten by all, he was left to fade away. But God remembered Joseph, took him out of the deep dungeon and placed him to sit right beside the King of Egypt.

In Egypt he became ruler of the land next to the King himself. And for seven years, by using His God-given wisdom and God's direction, he saved the people of Egypt from famine along with many others including his father's household.

Every bad thing that happened to Job and Joseph worked out for good in the end. Yet, during the occurrences of such like incidences in our lives, I am sure none of us would choose to or be willing to give God thanks for any of them. But, God works it all out for good.

God is the One who allowed the drunk to be a drunk, a menace to society and a wife beater. Is it a good thing? No! Are we to give thanks to God for him and his drunkenness? Yes.

We can choose to give thanks to God for allowing these circumstances. Why? Because God is Sovereign, and He has allowed that man to be who he is in his own free will that he possesses.

Who knows how God is using his drunkenness to cause the entire family, friends and perhaps foes, to draw closer to God. Perhaps this very thing is causing them to fast and pray; to intercede on his behalf in order to see God liberate him. It could well be that they will see their own lives transformed because of it all.

Transformed by Sufferings of Others

Do you think that drunks wake up happy after they have beaten up the person they love most? Are they glad that they frightened and upset their children, and that they are a hazard to society? They spend all their time, energy and resources on alcohol, do you think that they are glad about that? I do not think so.

I think that they suffer more than we can ever dream or imagine. I believe that one reason why they go back to drinking is to kill the pain. And they get caught up so deeply into it that there seems to be no way out.

They bury their shame in their drinking and hide their faces from their family. They become isolated and shunned, immersed in inferiority and shame, lonely and rejected. No one wants to be next to them. None of their family members want to talk to them or be nice to them.

They suffer, and many times God uses their sufferings to bring us closer to Him. He molds us and shapes us, builds fortitude and moral character into us, and prepares us for His use.

Because of the sufferings of others, we are benefited in the end.

Giving Thanks for All Things

Are we to give thanks then for *all things*? Even for the drunken father, the drug addicted son, the prostitute daughter, the relentless thief, and for others and their deeds? Yes we are!

God allows bad things, and causes them to work entirely for our good just like He allowed what seemed to be a bad thing two thousand years ago.

We need to give Him thanks for bad things as much as for good things, whatever they may be. God allowed them! He is sovereign! In His grace and mercy and great love, He allows bad things and works them out for our good.

It is hard for us to understand and accept this truth, because bad things are painful. And we do not want to be thankful for anything that causes pain because we believe that all bad things come from the devil.

We have been indoctrinated so much to believe that

bad things come from the devil that it is difficult for us to see that God allowed those things.

Take a look at Job for example, and see how God allowed bad things in his life. In the end good came out of it. Job was blessed above and beyond what he had before.

Joseph also was blessed, but the blessing was not for him alone. It also extended to Egypt, Israel, and the surrounding nations. All of this was God's great love in action.

"God's love for us can be accepted only by faith, just as we accept every other promise in the bible." Merlin R. Carothers, from his book, *Power in Praise*.

God is sovereign, and nothing happens without Him knowing about it. The devil could not do anything to Job without God saying, "You can do it."

The Bible says that not one sparrow falls to the ground without God knowing about it. It says that He is concerned about the lilies.

"Consider the lilies of the field, how they grow; they toil not, neither do they spin." Matthew 6:28

Alcoholism, drug addiction, carousing and reveling, adultery, fornication, and tons of other evil, God allowed many times in many lives. And then He caused the very things to bring the alcoholic, drug addict, adulterer and other evil doers on their knees before Him.

There He saved them, delivered them, and healed

them. And God allowed it all because *the person by his or her own free will chose to commit the evil.* God forces no one to do anything.

Loving God Who Allows Bad

Flavio Santos was visiting Toronto in 2003 when I met him. When he heard that the trip I had planned to Manaus, Brazil was cancelled, he invited me to Uberlândia, Minas, Gerais.

I knew that God was maneuvering the whole thing. However, I sought the Lord for confirmation before going to Uberlândia. It is in this City that I started Agua Viva– Living Water, and Igreja Cristo Exaltado–Christ Exalted Church. Perhaps one day I will tell the entire story.

It is now August 2005, and I have been traveling back and forth for the last two years between Canada and Brazil. This is the third trip and I usually spend six months there each time.

I have experienced many wonderful things here at the hand of God, and the following account is just one example. This took place one day in 2004.

On a Wednesday, I went to see nine-year-old Johnny in the Hospital. I prayed for him because he had cancer.

When I saw him, he was connected to intravenous and oxygen. His tummy was bloated, there was blood in his urine, and he was very weak.

His mother, with a look of despair, fatigue and hopelessness on her face was sitting in a chair beside his bed. She had been told by the doctors that he wasn't going to make it, and she looked as if she also had given up.

Jay Mooij who is like a father to me, said to me once, "*David, whenever you minister to people, have compassion on them. Jesus had compassion on the multitudes.*"

I have never forgotten his counsel. Jesus always had compassion on the crowds of people and healed them.

I said a few words of encouragement to John, laid my hands on his head and asked his Aunt Magna, who took me to see him, to read scripture. She read Psalm 103.

As his Aunt read, compassion like I had never felt before flooded my soul for the child and his mother. A great surge of force went through me, through my hands and to the boy. I prayed for him and then for his mother, encouraged them and promised to return.

When I returned a week later, the boy was breathing freely without the help of an oxygen mask. His tummy was back to normal, and there was no blood in his urine. He spoke with a smile on his face.

His mother also, though tired, was smiling. She had hope. All of John's organs were functioning normally and he was up and around on his own. Hallelujah!

Jesus still works miracles. Johnny received Jesus as

his personal Lord and Savior that day.

How can a loving God allow bad? How can He permit bad things to happen when He is so good? Why does He let evil occur in the lives of people that *He loves so much*? People whom He sent His Son to die for?

But this is it! *He loves us and that is why He sometimes allows bad.* Look at Jesus on the cross. Would you say that death on a cross is a good thing?

Cancer, diabetes, arthritis, aids, sickness and pain; God allows them all.

Looks Can Deceive You

Sometime after 11.00 p.m. Friday, October 12, 2001:

The door swung open. Sauntering over to the counter she ordered coffee. A large cup of coffee was placed before her and she paid for it. Picking it up with both hands, she leisurely walked over and gently placed the cup on a table and sat down.

With focused Filipina eyes she looked straight out the window. Slowly, she reached up to her hair and fixed her headband.

She was very pretty, maybe fifteen years of age and of small stature. She was about eight feet in front of me to my right, facing the window to my left.

Picking up the coffee cup with both hands, she slowly

brought it to her lips and took a sip.

She appeared to be calm, cool, and collected. She gave the impression that she was relaxed, at ease, and without a problem in the universe. She seemed to have the whole world in her hands, and as if time would stand still for her if she so wished.

Every so often she sipped from her coffee cup.

After a very short while, without notice, she switched tables and was sitting directly in front of us looking out of the other window.

The church service held in the recreation room of the apartment building where I live, had finished a while ago. We had come to the coffee shop for our regular cup of coffee.

I wasn't feeling like leaving home tonight, but I did anyway. I wanted to go to bed early because we had an outreach at another church the next day. But, God had an appointment with our young friend.

A short while after she came in and sat down, we got up to leave. I had with me two of the little "Daily Strength" booklets that are distributed by Scripture Gift Mission and decided to give one to her.

Donald Godfrey and his friend, thinking that I was behind them went out to the car. But, being moved by the Holy Spirit I headed over to the young lady. I walked just past her and stopped in front of her to her right. She looked up at me. I smiled, "I would like to give this to you."

"Oh, thank you," She reached out and took the booklet from my hand gratefully.

"Are you waiting for friends, or family?" I had no idea why I was asking her this question.

"Actually - right now, I need a family."

Suddenly, her voice was so sad. Her face turned pale, and her composure was totally changed. From someone who seemed to be carrying the whole world in her hands, she now seemed as if she needed someone to carry her.

"What do you mean?" I was really concerned.

"It's a long story," Her eyes began to fill up with tears as she replied.

"Tell me." I sat right down beside her without even asking.

There were no signs to indicate that here was a girl with a load of troubles. There was nothing that you could point to and say that she had problems.

She seemed happy, she smiled, and her face was bright. How would you have known that here was someone with major problems on her mind? Here was someone who desperately needed help?

I didn't know, and I couldn't tell. Not until I asked if she was waiting for friend or family did I find out the truth.

Since she was thirteen years old, she had been having problems with her parents. They didn't want her to work after school hours and they didn't want her to hang out with friends. Perhaps there is a lot more that she didn't tell me.

However, about three months ago her mother had told her to leave. She wasn't welcome in the house anymore. So she left, and had been staying with her friend. This other girl's parents had received her and welcomed her.

As she told me her story, tears flowed down her face. I am unsure how I did it, but with all my strength I kept my composure. My heart wept for her. I handed her a paper tissue and she gently wiped away her tears, but that didn't stop the flow. She desired so much to be with her family.

Most people were going to be with their family this weekend to celebrate Thanksgiving. And the thought of it perhaps caused her to yearn even more for her own Mom and Dad.

Her plan was to go to them that night with hopes that they would accept her and receive her into the family again. I didn't know what to say to her and I whispered to the Lord to give me the words. I told her to tell her Mom that she loved her and that she missed her.

We shared for a while and I encouraged her the best way I could. Then I prayed with her that she would find favor with her Mom, and that there would be reconciliation.

I was then urged by Holy Spirit to talk with her

about receiving Christ as her Savior and Lord. So I asked her if she knew what the term "born again" meant. She didn't.

She had heard the term "born again," but didn't understand its meaning. So I explained to her that Christ died for all of us two thousand years ago. That it is through Him that we have access to Heaven and through no one else. Thus we need to receive Him as our Lord and Savior.

When you ask Him, He will forgive you all of your sins, come live in your spirit, transform it and make you a new person. And that is what it means to be born again.

I then asked her if she wanted to be born again, and she replied, "Yes!"

Right there that very night, she prayed and asked Jesus into her heart to be her Lord and Savior. She was born again! Praise God.

God filled her with His peace, the angels in Heaven rejoiced, and a new name was written down for her in the *Lamb's Book of Life.*

A great big change took place in her right before my eyes. She shone more brightly than before and there was a rich smile on her face. She was so full of gratitude, and kept thanking me, saying, "I didn't know if anyone was going to talk with me."

All around us are hurting people who are lost and alone just like this beautiful young girl. Many are dying and going to hell. Make an effort to be aware of those around you and reach out to them.

You never know what person; what Christina or Sara or Margaret or Ron or Jim, might be sitting there next to you, hoping that someone would talk with them.

My new friend went home with fresh hope to help her speak to her parents.

"And He said to them, 'Go into all the world, and preach the gospel to all creation.'" Mark 16:15

" . . . And he who is wise wins souls." Proverbs 11: 30 (NAS)

"Your testimony is a soul winning tool!!!"

Do you see, how bad can work out for good?

Choices We Make

Sometimes, choices we make bring trouble and difficulties into our lives. And God stands back and allows those things to take their course. But at the same time, He works in the very situation to bring about good for us.

Reverend Angus Nicholson and his wife Rose were my pastors at one time and are very good friends of mine. I learned much from them. One day, Pastor Nicholson said to me, "Dave, whenever you have to make a decision in a situation, make the decision."

He didn't mean for me not to seek God in situations, but that I shouldn't hesitate for the rest of my life before making a decision. He told me that if I make a decision, I will soon find out if it was good or bad.

This advice has helped me on many occasions.

Many times in the midst of difficulties and troubles, you might cry out; "Why God?" That is because you do not see the hand of God in your predicament. You are so physically, mentally and emotionally involved in your problem and in what you are experiencing that you do not see Him move. You get so entangled that you are unable to think or see clearly.

This is when you need to practice Proverbs 3:5,

"Trust in the Lord with all your heart and lean not on your own understanding, but in all your ways acknowledge Him and He will direct your paths."

Do you have a proud, arrogant person in your life? Is there anyone who frustrates you to the brink of explosion with his or her offensive attitude and behavior? Are there people in your life who treat you as if you are nothing and nobody?

Can you thank God for them? Are you rejected and despised? Can you thank God for that? You should.

In and through these people and in all these things, God is working out good for you. In the end He brings you closer to Him. Ultimately, He builds character and strength in you and makes you a better person. And finally, He blesses you beyond anything you could ever dream or imagine.

"For when we were yet without strength, in due time Christ died for the ungodly. For scarcely for a righteous man will one die: yet peradventure for a good man some would even dare to die. But God commendeth His love towards us, in that, while we were yet sinners, Christ died for us. Much more then, being now justified by His blood, we shall be saved from wrath through Him. For if, when we were enemies, we were reconciled to God by the death of His Son, much more, being reconciled, we shall be saved by His life. And not only so, but we also joy in God through our Lord Jesus Christ, by whom we have now received the atonement."
Romans 5:6–11

"Giving thanks unto the Father, which hath made us meet to be partakers of the inheritance of the saints in light . . ." Colossians 1:12

"In every thing give thanks: for this is the will of God in Christ Jesus concerning you." 1Thessalonians 5: 18

Chapter 6

GRACE UNBOUNDED

"God's WORD is a mirror. If you look into it long enough, you will see yourself."

Agony of Guilt

Torrents of tears pour from blood shot eyes as you cast yourself to the floor. On bended knees you beg for forgiveness. Your heart pounds like a jackhammer hitting the pavement.

Terror holds you as if at any moment you might be cast into hell to suffer for all eternity. Fear has fastened its teeth on your heart like those of a bulldog and sweat drenches you. Shame has overwhelmed you and fright threatens you.

You want to hide your face from the Lord like Moses in the desert. To look up is as hard as to hold up arms that have been lifting hundred pound weights all day long. Facing your Maker at this moment is not easy.

You cower behind folded hands, your face tucked between your knees. Visions of angels coming to grab you by the neck and throw you into the lake of everlasting fire engulf your mind.

You tell God everything you have done. You plead and beg forgiveness for every detail that you can remember.

Nothing must be left out. Nothing must be forgotten and every sin must be totally forgiven. You are not going to sin again. You are going to fight next time. You will not give up and you will not succumb.

Oh, that God would take you back. That He would free you from this evil, this addiction, this tormenting occurrence of wickedness. That He would make you strong. That He would not look upon your sins.

You say with David, "Lord I have sinned against You and against You only have I done this wrong. Do not reward me according to my sin."

Your iniquity seems the biggest the world has ever known. You know that you know better. It doesn't matter how big or how small a sin you have committed, it's just that you have committed wickedness, and you feel wretched and miserable. You do not want to feel this way ever again.

Remorse, shame, unworthiness, fear and a feeling of being lost, torment you. Guilt overwhelms you.

> "Against thee, thee only, have I sinned, and
> done this evil in thy sight . . . Hide thy face
> from my sins, and blot out all mine iniquities."
> Psalm 51:4 and 9

It isn't important what sin you have committed, big or small. It doesn't matter for what length of time you have been involved in it. It is destructive and it separates.

You can walk around for years with guilt also for something done when you were a child. Weighted down with this burden you can be removed from others whom you have wronged. That others may have forgotten about what you have done doesn't matter. You haven't forgotten.

A person can become isolated and distant in relationship and behavior.

Every time that you remember the act, the word or words you have spoken, or the unjust treatment to others you feel ashamed. When you recall the stories you told about them, and the time that you walked away from helping them, it causes you pain.

It is difficult to face those you have hurt, to relate with them and to look them in the eye. There is no rest as you ponder how you could have avoided such mistakes.

However, the unrest, the upset stomach, the feeling

of guilt and shame doesn't go away. It hurts!

As time passes, you learn to live with shame, remorse, inferiority, low self-esteem, and fear of failure. Whenever you are faced with the same or similar situation, you are afraid that you will fail again. You are frightened that you will make the same old mistake.

You run from situations or from people. You become more and more isolated. Relationships are lost and friends and family are avoided.

The Past Haunts

"As long as you hold on to the past God cannot give you your future"

Guilt of the past has a way of popping up every so often. It usually confronts you when you have committed some other sin and you are feeling guilty. Suddenly all the wrongs you have done to others in the past seem to unearth themselves. Somehow it seems they have received rain and sunshine. They are shooting up like unwanted dandelions.

I did something once to my younger brother when he was about ten years old. I love him very much and would never dream of hurting him, but I did.

As the older child in my family there has been this gift or calling - downright burden I call it - to make sure that the younger siblings were growing up on the straight and narrow. And where that came from I am not so sure.

One day, my brother said a dirty word according to our next-door neighbor - his friend. I believed his friend and not my brother. And I punished him, humiliating him in front of the neighbor.

My biggest mistake was that I didn't give him the shadow of the doubt. And the second mistake was humiliating him in front of his friend. I listened to a stranger and not my own brother.

It doesn't mean that strangers lie or we are to always believe our own family.

Regrettably, I didn't trust my brother enough to tell me the truth. He was only a child and I didn't actually hear him say a bad word.

I should have shown him that I trusted him to tell me the truth. It would have been better if I had demonstrated that I would not believe someone else over him. I am sure that I would have had better results. He would have loved me more for it and would have done his best to make me more proud of him. His life would have been better and so too would have been mine.

I lived with that guilt and shame for about fifteen years. It was only when I sat down with my brother, told him what I had done, and asked his forgiveness that I was set free from the shame and guilt. He didn't even remember the incident.

However, I remembered it for many years, and it hurt.

It still bothers me sometimes when I remember, like right now. Because I love my brother very much and I hurt him once.

Guilt does this to us. It has this effect. It separates us from others and God. Some people shun God because of guilt. They do not return to church or stay in contact with other church members.

Somehow they have this feeling that church people have scanners or ex-ray vision. And every time they sin, they feel that Christians can see right through them and know exactly what they have done.

Forgiveness Heals

There is only one remedy for guilt and that is *forgiveness.* Forgiveness is the only thing that relieves one from the feelings of guiltiness and shame. When you have received pardon you are able to face the people you have wronged with a clear conscience. It is only after absolution that you are able to have healthy relationships with them.

Guilt must be removed. Shame must be dispelled. Forgiveness is the medicine. It is the only remedy. Confess your wrong, and receive your pardon.

When Others Wrong You

Most people who are depressed are often carrying burdens

of the past; burdens of wrong they have done or crimes that others have committed against them. To be free from this heaviness is to confess the sin and receive forgiveness for it. Or pardon those who have wronged you.

The evil others have done to you carries with it feelings of unworthiness. Lack of acceptance, low self-esteem and inferiority are all part of it. To get rid of these is to forgive those who have wronged you; *whether they ask for forgiveness or not.* After you pardon them, you are able to receive healing and be delivered from all the unworthiness, feelings of non-acceptance, low self-esteem and inferiority.

Sometimes people make mistakes and are not even aware of their wrong doings. Often they act wrongly with the belief that they are doing right. It is not always that people deliberately and spitefully hurt you. In some cases they unknowingly commit evil against you.

I am not trying to put blame on the wrong party. But hopefully you will understand that when you may be thinking that certain ones hate you, they do not necessarily hate you, nor have they really wanted to hurt you.

Perhaps they do not even know that they have committed a crime against you. They may not even know that they have caused you pain.

There are people who may have hurt you just like I hurt my brother. And they are probably living with a sense of shame. In pride not wanting to face you, they are doubly suffering for their mistakes. They need absolution. They need to be set free. And for you to be free is to forgive. You have no choice but to forgive them. Because in forgiveness lies true freedom.

> Mark 11:25, 26, "And when ye stand praying, forgive, if you have ought against any: that your Father also which is in heaven may forgive you your trespasses. But if ye do not forgive, neither will your Father which is in heaven forgive your trespasses."
>
> Matthew 6: 12, "And forgive us our debts, as we forgive our debtors."

There isn't anywhere in the Bible where Jesus says that anyone who has sinned against you, *must* come to you *first* before you can forgive him or her. *He says you must forgive others before you can be forgiven.*

Those who have wronged you or whom you feel have committed a crime against you, *must be pardoned by you.* And then your Father in Heaven will forgive you.

Note that Jesus said, "Your Father, which is in Heaven." This signifies that He is speaking to His children, those who have received Christ Jesus as Lord and Savior. And as children He says to us:

> "But I say unto you, love your enemies, bless them that curse you, do good to them that hate you, and pray for them which despitefully use you, and persecute you; that ye may be the *children of your Father* which

is in heaven . . ." Matthew 5:44 and 45

Sin Dilemma

Sin has the same effect on us in relation to our Heavenly Father. It separates us from Him. The voice of God echoes in the branches as He calls for repentance!

If you haven't confessed your sins to Him and received pardon, you will try to conceal yourself from Him. You will feel guilty, shameful and afraid. You will hide like Adam in the garden. And heaviness will linger over you like a morning fog after a rainy night. Let the Son shine upon it and it will disappear.

The greatest thing that you can do is confess your sin to your Father God. He will forgive you. And you will be free from the feelings of guilt, shame, unworthiness, low self-esteem, inferiority and fear. Let the light of Jesus shine upon your sin. It will disappear.

> 1 John 1: 9, "If we confess our sins, he is faithful and just to forgive us our sins, and to cleanse us from all unrighteousness."

The quandary of sin has hounded humanity on a grand scale since the fall of man. It also posed a dilemma for God. It had to be dealt with, removed and forgotten. It forms a dividing wall between God and His beloved children. He had to deal with it once and for all.

Iniquity keeps people from having fellowship with

God. Every time that God remembers evil there is the call for punishment. The law requires penalty for crimes and so sin had to be dealt with once and for all.

> Psalm: *139:1*, "O Lord, thou hast searched me, and known me. Thou knowest my downsitting and mine uprising, thou understandest my thoughts afar off. Thou compassest my path and my lying down, and art acquainted with all my ways."

God saw the effect of wickedness and what it did to His people in the Old Testament. He knew that evil had to be dealt with on such a level that man would *not be hindered by it*. He would not be obstructed from approaching his Heavenly Father for worship and intimate relationship.

Sin posed a great problem for God and His children. They commit evil, they are guilty and ashamed, and they hide from Him. He gets angry and He punishes them. This game of hide and seek must be stopped.

The heart of man is conceited and full of deceit. It had to be changed. God saw that man in his own strength and ability was unable to change his own heart or ways. Man needed help in a monumental way.

"The heart is deceitful above all things, and desperately wicked . . ." Jeremiah 17: 9

There was only one way out, one solution that would enable man to *approach God unhindered and uninhibited by sin*. God needed to facilitate this relationship by providing the answer, but how?

The solution was to *change the heart of man and give him the ability to have unhindered communion with God.* The plan was to create a way that any man who sinned would be able to repent and be forgiven of his sins, have them removed and forgotten, and immediately receive restored fellowship.

> 1 John 1: 9, "If we confess our sins, he is faithful and just to forgive us our sins, and to cleanse us from all *unrighteousness.*"

What then is unrighteousness? If it is what we have to be cleansed of, it then is unclean isn't it? It makes one unclean. It is in direct connection to wickedness and is the product of it. It must be removed.

Unrighteousness is *not having right standing* with God. It means that your relationship with God is hindered and broken. It is damaged and needs repair. You are like Adam in the Garden of Eden, needing forgiveness of sins by the sacrifice of The Lamb.

Righteousness

What is righteousness? Righteousness is having *right standing* with God. It means that to God, you are as one who has done no wrong. You are as one who has committed no sin. You are clean and are accepted by God. You are honorable, highly esteemed, virtuous, moral and just. You have unhindered, unrestricted, open, direct, free and intimate relationship with God your Father.

This is where God desires each and every one of us to be. And He made the way for that to occur.

What does it really mean to be righteous? What does it mean to have right standing with God?

2nd Corinthians 5:21, "For he hath made him
to be sin for us, who knew no sin; that we might be
made the righteousness of God."

I like the word here, *made. It defines clearly that it is all of God and not of humanity* which is very important. *He made*, that is, God made you *His righteousness.*

Every time I meditate on this thought it awes me. *It is a fascinating and an awesome contemplation that God made me His righteousness.*

What is His righteousness?

The Greek word for righteousness is *dikaiosune* and means *right-doing*. When it says that God has made you His righteousness, it means that He has made you His right doing. *He has made you right and proper.*

Think of God's right doing. What is God's right doing? Everything that God does is *good* and *right*. Every act of God is proper and just. God is good and what He does is *good* and *right*. God made you His right doing.

It is an amazing thought that overwhelms the mind.

He made you to have right standing with Him. He

recreated you in Christ to be as if you have done no wrong. He caused you to be present before him without anything evil, malicious, immoral, wicked or of fault. *You are clean in His eyes.*

Therefore you are in right relationship with Him.

That means then that He accepts you. He receives your prayers. Your petitions and requests are heard and answered by Him. He removed the hindrance (unrighteousness - sin) between you and Him. There is no wall of sin blocking your relationship.

There is free and clear communication. There is intimate relationship, there is friendship, there is love, and there is fellowship.

Right doing is described in the Thesaurus as right and proper, right from the start, righteousness, righteously and righteousness.

Righteous is described as virtuous, moral, good, just, blameless, upright, honorable, honest, respectable and decent.

Righteousness is described as morality, virtue, justice, decency, uprightness, honesty, and integrity.

In some languages like Portuguese, the Greek word *dikaiosune* is translated justification. *Justification* is described in the Thesaurus as *good reason, rationalization and excuse.* God did not make us an excuse or good reason. He made us righteousness in Christ.

In the King James Bible, the Greek words *dikaiosis* and *dikaioso* are translated as justification. *Dikaiosis* and *dikaioso* means *God declares me free.*

Dikaiosune is different from the two words above. It has a deeper and greater meaning. It is translated *righteousness* in the King James Bible as in 2nd Corinthians 5: 21.

It means more than just good reason, rationalization or excuse. *Dikaiosune* (righteousness) is saying exactly what you are, *and not what excuse you have for being recreated in Christ as the righteousness of God.*

What then has God made you when it says that He made you His righteousness in Him (Christ)?

It means that He has made you right and proper, right from the start. He made you righteous, righteously and righteousness. He made you to be virtuous, moral, good, just, blameless, upright, honorable, honest, respectable and decent. He doesn't just declare you free, but He also gave you *His attributes.* I can hear you shouting hallelujah!

We see therefore that without this grand change in man, he cannot have deep and intimate relationship with God. God did for him what he couldn't do for himself.

> "I am crucified with Christ: nevertheless I live; yet not I, but Christ liveth in me: and the life which I now live in the flesh I live by the faith of the Son of God who loved me and gave himself for me." Galatians 2: 20

So your old life has been done away with. You are changed; transformed from one life into another; your life is integrated into the life of Christ. And that new life is righteousness!

"Therefore if any man be in Christ, he is a new creature: old things are passed away; behold all things have become new." 2nd Corinthians 5:17

Are you in Christ? Then you are a new person. You are not the old self that you use to be. You are changed. *You are a new creation;* the righteousness of God.

". . . much more they which receive abundance of grace and of the gift of righteousness shall reign in life by one, Jesus Christ." Romans 5: 17

As you can see, this *righteousness is a gift and is received by faith* the very moment that you accept Christ as your Lord and Savior. It is not something that you make happen by good deeds. It is not something that you work for. It is received freely by faith. And it is yours because of God's unbounded and abundant grace.

" . . . But we have the mind of Christ." 2nd Corinthians 2:16

So then in dealing with the sin dilemma, God transformed you through Christ even to giving you the mind of Christ. This enables you to think as He thought and to be able to relate to God at the same level as Christ when He was physically on the earth.

However, to think like Christ constantly you must fill your mind with the words of God. Jesus was full of the word of God. You now have the ability to serve Him with a mind transformed by the word of God to His glory and honor.

Revelation

It was a gorgeous morning - sunny with clear skies, but cool; quite tranquil. My very good friend Luigi Cianfarani and I were at Georgian Bay. Early that morning he waded out to a rock that stuck out of the water, sat on it and read his Bible.

"Dave, Dave! Come here! Come Here! Look what it says!" He was standing on the rock and waving at me, motioning for me to go to him. I had to wade over to him in the freezing cold water of the lake. And he wouldn't tell me what it was until I reached him. He was ecstatic!

"Save now, I beseech thee, o lord: o lord, I beseech thee, send now prosperity." Psalm 118:25

This word was a revelation to him. For the first time in his life he truly recognized that God really wants to prosper us. He was having a whole new experience in God. And I hope that you are having the same kind of an experience right now.

Chapter 7

OVERCOMING LOVE

"The mind is a garden of beauty and riches, if, one can conceive it."

Man's Struggle With Weakness

"I have a great big bad weakness and I carry it everywhere I go. I cannot run from it, hide from it, conceal it, or deny it. I cannot put it away, give it up or make it go away. It is constantly with me. It burdens me, causes me much discomfort, pain, and sadness.

This is a continuous unwanted battle that I fight every day. It is a torment and a never-ending load. Many others are hurt by it as well. How I wish that it would go away.

I wish that I never had it, had to put up with it, or fight against it each day. It is my biggest enemy. It regularly wants its own way, desires to do its own thing, and demands that its cravings be satisfied.

Who will set me free from this torment? Who will free me from this death that abides with me? Who will liberate me from this aggravation?"

Does this sound like you?

Under the harrowing strain of incessant conflict with unwanted habits, desires and cravings, you try to set yourself free. Carrying the weight of what people might think of you if they knew of your little secret, you are burdened with a constant losing battle.

You experience agonizing pain from running back to the thing day after day. You greatly desire to break free, but how?

There seems to be no hope. There seems to be no help. And no avenue comes into view that you may slip into and drive away.

Where can you go? Where can you hide? What can you do, but live with the embarrassing and shameful torment? Your hope is gone. Confidence is shaken, depression steps in, and sleepless nights take over.

It is not easy to hide from yourself. Maybe it's easy to hide from other people, but from yourself? What will you do? How can you be freed?

Deadly Companion

Alcohol has been his companion and friend for many years. They have shared countless hours of tender moments. Many days were spent mutually meditating. And much time was used up contemplating the future.

To seek divorce from this long time pal is not easy. After all they have spent many long hours together.

Ah, the sweet embraces; the often glorious flights taken together. What a friend? What a companion? None were more close or endearing; a bosom buddy so dependable.

To be separated from such a friend is unthinkable. Oh, how can it be?

When no one spoke to you, when no one cared enough to visit, and when no one phoned or sent a letter, your good old friend, "bottle of booze," was there. When no one thought about you, your alluring companion was always nearby.

Oh, the torment, the agony, and the wretchedness of letting go.

Troubled soul, tormented mind, and broken body are what this wonderful friend leaves you with. Divided homes, distraught and destroyed children, emotionally damaged spouse and broken marriage. Lost and forever smashed.

Why remain in this relationship? Why persist in this

association? Why remain in this boat?

It is time to jump ship. It is the opportune moment to change course. Now is when to turn around and find a new friend.

There is a friend who sticks closer than a brother. He never will leave you nor forsake you. He is no respecter of persons. He does not demand his own way. He by no means forces his way upon you. And He does not pressure you to do anything that you do not want to do.

That old friend; *the bottle,* is no respecter of persons either. But when he takes charge, he has his way. You lose control of your life.

You do not do as you please, but as he pleases. You do not do what you want to do with a clear conscious mind. You are led by him on a leash that leads to destruction.

The strength of his grip is greater than the force of a pit-bull's bite. Once his hold is on he does not let go. The power of his hold, the bitterness of his bite, and the pain it gives, are everlasting. Destruction, apathy, pain, madness, loneliness, blindness and shame are all part of the reward.

There are so many people in similar conditions. So many individuals are struggling with all kinds of bond-ages. All types of chains are around their necks, and they are unable to free themselves. They need Jesus!

When a person is held in the grips of Satan, there is only one remedy. *And that is salvation!* Only Christ can set you free from the devil's hold. Life in Christ is the answer.

You have that life since Christ is your Lord and Savior. And you can make a difference in the lives of those around you.

The Battle Was Won

Paul the Apostle described having a "thorn in his flesh," a battle within him. He recognized the problem and he didn't know how he would be free. However, one day he received the answer.

He realized that there was a solution. It was revealed to him that he didn't have to fight as hard as he thought he would have to. He didn't have to battle the thorn, but embrace his new life of strength and power in Christ.

> "And he said unto me, My *grace is sufficient* for thee: for my strength is made perfect in weakness. Most gladly therefore will I rather glory in my infirmities, that the power of Christ may rest upon me." 2nd Corinthians 12:9

He wrote to the Roman Jews knowing where they stood in their own righteousness. That is, in their own wisdom and understanding; a people who lived to serve the Law. He needed to clearly show them that it is not the law or letter that makes a man free, but that it is Christ who sets the captive free.

"For the law of the *Spirit of life* in Christ Jesus hath made me *free* from the law of sin and death." Romans 8:2,

The *Spirit of life*, which is the life of Christ who is in you, is what sets you free.

> "Therefore if any man be in Christ, he is a new creature: old things are passed away; behold, all things are become new."
> 2nd Corinthians 5:17

> "For in Christ Jesus neither circumcision availeth any thing, nor uncircumcision, but a *new creature*." Galatians 6:15

Observe therefore, that it is this new life in Christ that sets a person free.

You In Christ

> "*I am crucified* with Christ: nevertheless I live; yet not I, but Christ liveth in me: and the life which I now live in the flesh I live by the faith of the Son of God, who loved me, and gave himself for me." Galatians 2:20

> "Knowing this, that our *old man is crucified* with him, that the body of sin might be destroyed, that henceforth we should not serve sin." Romans 6:6

As a born again person you were crucified with Christ.

Therefore the life you now live, you live it in Christ. Since you were crucified you no longer live, Christ lives!

"For to me to live is Christ, and to die is gain." Philippians 1:21.

Where does that leave you?

> "Know ye not, that so many of us as were baptized into Jesus Christ were baptized into his death? Therefore we are buried with him by baptism into death: that like as Christ was raised up from the dead by the glory of the Father, even so we also should walk in *newness of life*." Romans 6:3, 4

Well, it leaves the old you buried! You were crucified with Christ, and you died with Him. You were buried with Him, and rose again with Him. The new "you" in Christ is alive and full of the resurrection power of the Spirit of God.

When the Spirit of God resurrected Christ's body from the dead, you were resurrected. When Jesus walked out of the tomb, you walked out of your tomb. You are alive in Christ *and full of His life!*

What does this really mean?

It means that you have "put on Christ." There was an exchange of identity. You have become a new creature. "Old things are passed away, behold all things have become new."

You are a new person. You have a new identity.

When you received Christ as your Lord and Savior, you participated in His death and resurrection.

How come?

He died in your stead. He took your place on the cross. He paid the price for your sins. Therefore, when He died you died. When he was resurrected, you were resurrected with Him into life everlasting!

"Jesus saith unto him, I am the way, the truth, and the life: no man cometh unto the Father, but by me." John 14:6

Jesus is the way, the door, the portal into Heaven. As you embraced Him on the cross, you were translated into Heaven. You were removed from this world to that world, from the powers of darkness to the powers of light, from death and destruction to life everlasting.

You were taken from the hands and the kingdom of Satan and placed into the hands and the kingdom of God.

Where does that leave you?

You are left seated at the right hand of Father God in Christ Jesus your Lord and Savior.

"And hath raised us up together, and made us sit together in heavenly places in Christ Jesus." Ephesians 2:6

What then is left for you to do?

"For to me to live is Christ, and to die is gain." Philippians 1:21

It is for you now to live as Christ lived, think as Christ

thought, speak as Christ spoke, and act as Christ acted.

> "Then saith he to Thomas, reach hither thy finger, and behold my hands; and reach hither thy hand, and thrust it into my side: and be not faithless, but believing."
>
> John 20:27

Believe the truth of the word of God! Doubt no longer, believe.

Power In Christ's Resurrection

"Verily, verily, I say unto you, He that believeth on me, the works that I do shall he do also; and greater works than these shall he do; because I go unto my Father." John 14:12

Do you believe that you can do the works of Christ?

If you believe, knowing that it is His life in you now, you can do the works of Christ. You can place your hands on the sick and say, "In the name of Jesus Christ be healed!" and that person will be healed. You can say to demons, "Come out of that person in the name of Jesus Christ!" and they will come out.

Colin Stephenson moved to Canada some years ago from Brazil. He wanted to do business there and invited me to travel with him. It was April of 1993 and we went to Rio de Janeiro.

There, in the month of May, I preached my very first

sermon. And we didn't do any other business! This began my travels to distant lands. Colin and I later became great friends.

Doing The Works of Christ

One day, I was casting out a demon spirit and out of the mouth of the demon possessed person came these words, "Get out of here! Get out of here!"

I calmly replied, "No one is getting out of here devil, but you. You come out of this woman in the name of Jesus Christ. You do not speak or make a fuss." Something close to that is what I said.

In a moment of time the woman was lying in her bed as if she was dead. I gently patted her on her face and she opened her eyes and began to weep. She begged me not to leave her all alone.

I then prayed with her and comforted her with the fact that Jesus is with her and remains with her after I leave.

You can do the very same thing in the name of Jesus Christ. You have the authority in Christ's name. You represent Him on this earth.

"For it is God which worketh in you both to will and to do of his good pleasure." Philippians 2:13

Knowing this fact changes everything. You realize that you can place your hands on the sick and see them healed. You recognize that you can cast out demons. It is

Christ in you who does the work.

> "Now the God of peace, that brought again from the dead our Lord Jesus, that great shepherd of the sheep, through the blood of the everlasting covenant, make you perfect in every good work to do his will, *working in you* that which is well pleasing in his sight, through Jesus Christ; to whom be glory for ever and ever. Amen." Hebrews 13:20, 21

On another occasion I was in Manaus, Brazil. I was there for a month, and God was ministering healing everywhere I went.

There was a young boy who had asthma and he was suffering terribly both physically and emotionally. His grandmother brought him to Irauna's house where I was staying and asked that I would pray for him.

It was the same day or the day after I prayed for him, that my young friend took the vacuum and began to clean the carpet.

Now, that is not what an asthmatic child is supposed to do! Dust is not a friendly companion to asthmatic people. Grandma, eager to save the boy from harm, asked him over and over to leave the cleaning and to do his home work. After three separate tries, she realized that he was healed. She left him alone.

"Then Peter said, Silver and gold have I none; but such as I have give I thee: In the name of Jesus Christ of

Nazareth rise up and walk." Acts 3:6

You too can say like Peter, "Silver and gold, I do not have. Weakness, poverty and shame I do not have. Sin, sickness and death, I do not have."

You can say, "I give you what I have. I give you life, health, prosperity, abundance, serenity, healing, deliverance, peace and joy. I give you Christ!"

What is left for you now is to live. What is left for you now is to manifest your new identity.

During this same visit to Manaus, I was praying for the sick to be healed. It was someone's birthday and we had a healing service by the pool. Imagine that!

At the end of the night, when everyone that had need of healing had received healing, a certain woman arrived. We had been waiting for her. She had an enlarged aorta and had been to the doctors, had exams taken, and was suffering pain.

As soon as she arrived, I placed my hands on her and prayed for her to receive healing. Afterwards, I asked her to return to the doctor and get new exams done. She said to me, "Pastor, I will go to the doctor because you asked me to. But, I know I am healed! I have no more pain!"

Two weeks later I was on the phone with Irauna's wife, Andrea. She told me that the lady had exams taken, and she is completely healed!

You can do the same! All things are possible to those who believe.

You Measure Up

In my travels to Brazil I have observed something tremendous among non-traditional Presbyterians. They have more openness to the moving of Holy Spirit, more so than many traditional Presbyterians I have met in Brazil.

But, most of all I have observed a tranquility in them that I have not seen in modern-day evangelicals. And I have traveled to a few countries. I have had the opportunity to observe Christians on a large scale.

I am not sure why, but these non-traditional Presbyterians seem to be more at ease with their relationship with God than many other Christians that I have observed. Don't they spend time in prayer and seek God like most of us? Sure they do! But they seem to be more confident in their relationship with the Lord.

Take for example Pastor Lúcio dos Reis Oliveira. He pastors the Fifth Presbyterian Church which is the largest in Uberlândia, Minas Gerais. He is a dear friend of mine and traveled with me to Canada in October of 2005.

He is a man of prayer, and you will find him praying alone for about an hour every morning in his church office. He was a great blessing to some of the Pentecostal churches in Toronto. They recognized the anointing of God in his life, and the Lord used him powerfully.

Pastor Lúcio is someone whom I believe is content with his relationship with God. This contentment doesn't make him sit back and not seek God's face every morning. But, it does cause him to be at ease with his Maker and allow Him to govern his life and work through him as He pleases.

Some other great friends of mine; Remi, his wife Lucia, his daughters Sara and Thaiza, and Remi Humberto their son, are also wonderful examples of this type of relationship. They demonstrate the same tranquility.

Don't they have problems like other people? Sure they do!

So often we have sat down together and shared, prayed and sought God for His intervention in matters. But they have such a calm way of going on with life that is so important for all of us to take notice of.

What have I observed?

They do not try to measure up to others or reach a certain standard or level for God. They simply serve Him. They live their lives one day at a time knowing that their lives are in Christ, that He is King and Governor, and they let him rule.

Sara is now married to Junior, and Thaiza to Wellington, and I am already seeing the same exemplified lives in them.

Another excellent family that I have had the wonderful pleasure to observe is Dr. Irauna Jacob's family. He and his wife Andrea, daughters Luana and Naiana, and their son Italo, have been a tremendous blessing to me. Italo was my official translator while in Manaus and it is in their home that I stayed while there.

I have noticed the same type of relationship with Christ in them as I have seen in Remi's family. They serve God in tranquility, and are an example to many.

My observation is that they too do not fight to reach a certain standard in God, but humbly seek the Lord in relationship and worship.

They are non-traditional Presbyterians of the Central Presbyterian Church of Manaus in Brazil. Pastor José João Mesquita is their pastor and has one of the largest boat ministries I know of. They minister to poor people living on the banks of the rivers of the Amazon. I have been on many trips on one of their Riverboats.

I have seen such a great love for each other in these two families that I have not seen in many other families.

Like these wonderful friends of mine *you do not have to strive to measure up for God.* He already brought you to the level you need to be at, which is, "Christ in you, the hope of glory."

Your life is hidden in Christ. You do not have to try to measure up or reach a certain level for God's use. Holy Spirit who is in you is sufficient! He does the work. Let Him speak through you, act through you, and touch lives through you.

"In whom(Christ) are hid all the treasures of wisdom and knowledge." Colossians 2:3

"For ye are dead, and *your life is hid with Christ in God.*" Colossians 3:3

You Are Sanctified

One reason people try to measure up or reach a certain level in God is because they do not believe that they are clean enough, holy enough, or good enough. They do not believe that they have been made perfect and attempt to attain a higher level of excellence.

Most Christians believe that if they can get more of God, get closer to Him, or attain a higher level in Him, only then can they be used by Him. This is absolutely untrue!

The two most important things that Father looks for in you are obedience and faith. Obedience will keep sin out of your life and faith brings the provision.

"Praying in FAITH moves God's hands to meet needs."

Some people try to gain perfection by doing things, all kinds of things. They go to church more so than most people, spend hours doing good deeds, fast more than others, pray longer and louder than others, etc.

They become religiously motivated instead of

relationally moved. God is seeking relationship with you, not religiosity.

People do this because they do not understand two things: that *they are sanctified* and that they do measure up; *they are sufficient in Christ*!

They do not recognize that they are not being sanctified, but *have already been sanctified.*

The moment you receive Christ as Lord and Savior you are sanctified. This, they do not understand.

Sanctification measures you up on God's scale. You do not have to try to measure up to Him or reach a certain altitude for Him. All that He desires from you is relationship. Love Him!

What then is sanctification?

> "But we are bound to give thanks always to God for you, brethren beloved of the Lord, because God hath from the beginning chosen you to *salvation through sanctification of the Spirit* and belief of the truth:"
>
> 2 Thessalonians 2:13

The word sanctification means: A religious ceremony in which something is made holy - Easton's 1897 Bible Dictionary.

Sanctify-Verb

1) Render holy by means of religious rites.

2). Declare holy or pure or free from sin; "he left the

monastery purified."

Oxford English Dictionary Sanctify / sangktifi / verb (sanctifies, sanctified)

1) make or declare holy; consecrate.

2) make legitimate or binding by religious sanction.

3) free from sin.

4) give the appearance of being right or good.

derivatives *sanctification*, noun *sanctifier*.

origin Latin *sanctifi care*, from *sanctus* "holy."

> "Unto the church of God which is at Corinth, to them that are *sanctified* in Christ Jesus, called to be saints, with all that in every place call upon the name of Jesus Christ our Lord, both theirs and ours."
>
> 1st Corinthians 1:2
>
> "To the church (assembly) of God which is in Corinth, to those *consecrated and purified and made holy* in Christ Jesus, [who are] selected and called to be saints (God's people) . . ."
>
> 1st Corinthians 1:2 Amplified Bible

Pay close attention and you will see that the word translated "*sanctified*" in KJV is translated "consecrated and purified and made holy" in the Amplified Bible. And you will observe closely that it is all past tense. It is something that has occurred, not something that is going to occur.

> "And such were some of you: but *ye are washed*, but *ye are sanctified*, but *ye are justified* in the name of the Lord Jesus, and by the Spirit of our God." 1Corinthians 6:11

> "For both he that sanctifieth and they who are sanctified are all of one: for which cause he is not ashamed to call them brethren," Hebrews 2:11

> "For by one offering *he hath perfected* for ever them that are sanctified." Hebrews 10:14

> "Of how much sorer punishment, suppose ye, shall he be thought worthy, who hath trodden under foot the Son of God, and hath counted the blood of the covenant, wherewith *he was sanctified*, an unholy thing, and hath done despite unto the Spirit of grace?" Hebrews 10:29

There is a difference between Old Testament sanctification and New Testament sanctification.

In the Old Testament, a man took an animal to the Priest to be sacrificed for the man's sin. Upon accepting the sacrifice, God covered the sins of the man with the blood of the animal, and accepted him. He was then sanctified. Having his sins covered by the blood of bulls and goats, he was consecrated to God.

"By the which will we are sanctified through the

offering of the body of Jesus Christ once for all." Hebrews 10:10"

In the New Testament, God made the one time sacrifice of His only begotten Son Jesus Christ.

Upon accepting God's sacrifice of Jesus Christ, a person has his sins forgiven and washed away by Christ's blood, never to be remembered by God again. He is sanctified: consecrated to God, purified, and made holy. He is now new.

So then, in the Old Testament man made a sacrifice. In the New Testament God made the sacrifice.

In the Old Testament *God accepts a person's sacrifice* in order to receive and sanctify him.

In the New Testament *man accepts God's sacrifice* and he is automatically sanctified by Holy Spirit. He is consecrated, purified and made holy immediately. He is made a new creation instantly.

This creative work takes place in your spirit. You are then transformed daily in your mind by Holy Spirit: in your thinking, in what you say and in what you do. You then grow mentally, emotionally, in faith and in character to exemplify Christ outwardly.

Chapter 8

GOD'S DESIRE FOR YOU

"Great things come out of great relationships that are based on God's great love."

Victory in Knowing Christ

"Father, I have been contemplating. When you sent Me into the world to pay the price for the sins of creation, I did exactly that. As I sit here beside you, I think of how it is going to be when the children recognize their place in Your Kingdom. There will be such great change in the earth."

Father turns to Jesus with hands open in front of Him expressively.

"Son, if they would only understand. If they would

only grasp what it is to be My child and realize who they are in You. The world would be a better place!"

"I have left the facts with them. I told them what You told Me. I had it written for them to remember. I informed them that I will never leave them nor forsake them.

Some have received this truth and look at the wonderful things that are being done through them. When others of them comprehend the truth, they will break down the walls that keep them back and have them locked in."

Father turns toward Jesus, leans over, looks right into His eyes, and responds emphatically.

"If they would only grab a hold of the truth Son, and take their place! They would walk in the power that is theirs and overcome Satan."

After pausing for a moment, Jesus motioned with His hands. "I left with them this fact, that I am the vine and they are My branches. With that knowledge alone they should see that their strength is drawn from Me.

They are My arms, eyes, feet, mouth, and hands. They are My body. And all that I am, and all that I have flows in and through them."

He began to be more serious with a strong, explicit look on His face.

"Father, when they begin to grasp this truth, their lives will forever be changed. The power that flows in Me flows in them. The life that is in Me is in them. The Holy Spirit that raised Me from the dead resides in them.

I am the trunk. As the trunk of a tree gives food to the branches, likewise I give to them food, living water, strength, power, and everything that pertains to life and godliness."

The same definite enthusiastic expression emerges on Father's face.

"One day Son, they will recognize and receive it. And when they do, they will transform the world they live in!

They are going to break down partition walls! They are going to set captives free! They are going to cast out demons, heal the sick, make the lame walk, open blind eyes, raise the dead and heal all kinds of sick bodies. They will do miracles in Your name."

"They need to realize that I am in them and they are in Me. You and I are One, and together We are in them. They have been transformed in their spirit by Holy Spirit who lives in them."

Jesus also began to be more thrilled and enthusiastic. Motioning with His hands, He pointed to Father and to Himself from time to time.

"As I am seated here beside You Father, they are seated beside You!"

He folds His hands in front of Him, and Father puts His arm around His shoulder. His voice is lower now.

"That is right Son. And all they have to do is turn to

Me and say, 'Hello Father'!" Father smiles at Jesus. He nods His head in agreement, and smiles back.

"I will hear them and reach out and hug them just as I hug You."

Jesus lifts His head sideways toward Father and looks at Him. He opens His right hand in front of Him and motions as He speaks.

"This fact: their place here beside You in Me, is what they must realize. They simply need to take My word for what it is. What I told them is the exact and absolute truth."

Father shakes His head up and down in agreement.

"They should remember what I told Isaiah to write, that 'by Your stripes they are healed.' They wouldn't be sick like so many of them are."

"Yes Father, and Peter also wrote the very same thing! I shared with them through John that whatever they would ask in My name, I will do it for them." Jesus was more resolute at this point.

"You and I know Son, that not all of them will comprehend all of the truth. We want them to! We paid such a great price for them to be free from sin and sickness and Satan. Yet, some of them will not recognize it, but those who do will change the world they live in."

They were silent for a moment, and then Jesus began again.

"Paul revealed to them their righteousness in Me.

Many are yet to receive that truth."

"That is true Jesus." Placing His right hand on Jesus' left shoulder, Father God replied.

"It would be fantastic if they would recognize that they do not have to wait until they get here to become righteous. They must realize that they are righteous *now* and that is how I see them. I see them justified!

I want them to comprehend that I look at them through You. And when I look at them through You, I only see You. I do not see them in the way they see themselves.

They look with human eyes. You and I, Jesus, We see with Our spiritual eyes. We see things differently. Whenever they call upon Me and I turn to look at them, what do I see? I see You! Every time I respond to them I must go through You.

They must realize Son, that You paid the total price. You gave Your blood as ransom for them, and I do nothing without You."

Taking His hand off Jesus' shoulder, Father turned forward again.

"Yes Father, it is as You say. And if they call in My Name, You do hear and answer them. Not only do you hear and answer them, You answer them even before they call unto You. This You told them through Isaiah in chapter sixty five, verse twenty four of his book.

Likewise, if they call like You instructed them in

chapter thirty three, verse three of Jeremiah's book, You will indeed answer and show them great and mighty things. *That is exactly what You will do*!"

Turning again to Jesus, Father God gripped His left hand tightly in His and gazed into His eyes with great excitement and expectation.

"When My children realize Son, what great and mighty things I have already done for them; when they recognize that I have already supplied and prepared everything, and Our ministering angels are waiting to deliver these things to them, their lives and their world will completely change.

How dramatic and thrilling it will be for them. I want so much for them to see these truths!"

Releasing His hand, Father God turned forward again.

"David also left them word at Your bidding Father. He told them that I am their Shepherd and they will never lack."

Placing His hand on Father's right arm and causing Him to turn once again toward Him, Jesus continued.

"Father, I am in them and they are in Me; You are in Me and I am in You. Together we are in them. You have recreated them in their spirit to be like Me; to think like Me, to speak like Me and to act like Me. We have even given them My mind. I have been made wisdom to them.

Paul informed them that they would be able to do all things through Me.

Since I am the trunk which supplies their strength and power and all that they need, they can do the works that I did and greater works than those. And I am waiting patiently for them to do these things!"

Father nodded His head and placed his arm around Jesus' shoulder. He indicated with His left hand.

"Jesus, as soon as they act in the faith that We have given them - and they all have a measure - You will act through them. You have no other choice. You are in them and that faith moves You to act."

"Correct, Father!"

They both became silent again. Angels and other beings who were listening were discussing the topic in twos and threes. Heads were moving up and down, arms were crossed, some were pointing and motioning. There was discussion going on all around.

Remove The Veil

There is a veil that covers the eyes of most Christians today. Most are still walking around with it over them. They got married and forgot to take off the veil.

Some believe that on the day that Jesus comes back for His Body, they will attain a certain level, and then the veil will be removed.

The fact of the matter is that the ceremony is over! You are already married and need to remove the veil so that the glory of God might shine forth from you!

What is it that is keeping the veil on?

Two things: unbelief and lack of knowledge of God's word. Therefore the veil is a veil of unbelief which is derived from lack of knowledge of the word of God.

Moses wore a veil over his head after He came down from the mountain. The glory of God shone on his face so powerfully that he had to cover it.

However, when the glory was not as evident on his face anymore, he removed the veil.

This is a man who experienced the glory of God more so than most other men. But the glory that he experienced, did not remain with him as powerfully as when he was in God's presence the first time. He had no need for a veil afterwards.

What Moses experienced was a result of God's glory coming upon him. It affected him to such a degree that he had to cover it.

You have been and are being affected from the inside out. In you resides the One with this glory that caused Moses to wear a veil. And there is no necessity for you to put on a veil because you were called to shine for Jesus!

You are light. And that light is there to shine and

give brightness to the world around you. It is there to bring change and transform other lives.

Paul tells us in 2nd Corinthians that the ministry of Holy Spirit is more glorious than the glory of Moses. The ministry of righteousness which is the ministry of Holy Spirit exceeds more in glory.

> ". . . children of Israel could not stedfastly behold the face of Moses for the glory of his countenance; which glory was to be done away: How shall not the ministration of the spirit be rather glorious? For if the ministration of condemnation be glory, much more doth the *ministration of righteousness exceed in glory*. For if that which is done away was glorious, much more that which remaineth is glorious."
>
> 2nd Corinthians 3:7, 8, 9, 11

Christ never fades away. Therefore the glorious ministry of righteousness will also not disappear. But, the veil of Moses was removed in Christ.

". . . which veil is done away in Christ. Nevertheless when it (someone) shall turn to the Lord, the veil shall be taken away." 2nd Corinthians 3:14, 16

This veil was taken away in Christ because the law was fulfilled in Christ. The requirements of the Law were met in Him.

Therefore if the veil has been taken away in Christ,

the glory of Christ should be shining forth from you.

> "But we all, with open face beholding as in a glass the glory of the Lord, are changed into the same image from glory to glory, even as by the Spirit of the Lord."
>
> 2nd Corinthians 3:18

With the veil gone, we look in the mirror and we see the reflection of Christ. Our faces are not covered, but are open; meaning free of any veil.

This ministry of Holy Spirit is a transforming one. He shines in your heart and gives you revelations of the glory of God. This is the light of the gospel. You reflect the image of God.

I look at you and you reflect the glory of God. You look at me and you see the glory of God.

> "For God, who commanded the light to shine out of darkness, hath shined in our hearts, to give the light of the knowledge of the glory of God in the face of Jesus Christ."
>
> 2nd Corinthians 4:6

There has been a great change in the person who is born again of the Spirit of the Lord. Because of this, Paul does not look at any Christian in the flesh or according to the outside reflection. He looks at them in the spirit. Because in the spirit is the new creation. You were recreated in your spirit.

> "Wherefore henceforth know we no man after the flesh: yea, though we have known Christ after the flesh, yet now henceforth know we him no more. Therefore if any man be in Christ, he is a new creature: old things are passed away; behold, all things are become new." 2nd Corinthians 5:16, 17

Like the veil of Moses and the Law of Moses that passed away, so too your old life; your past, has passed away. You have become new–you have put on Christ. You are now recreated in His image and likeness, in your spirit. From now on you should and will shine forth with the glory of God. And even more so, as you develop and strengthen intimate relationship with your Maker–Father God.

So, remove the veil and let Christ shine forth from you.

Chapter 9

THE NEW YOU

"Your FUTURE does not depend on your past, but on what you believe in your heart."

Sitting by the way side has been the corner stone of my life. Begging has become my trade; loneliness my companion; dust, sweat and stench, my best friend.

I am taken to the corner every day to practice my trade. Lunch is brought to me. And in the evening, someone comes and takes me home.

The rain beats on me, the sun scorches me, and the wind blows dust and sand on me. Children call me names, idiots make fun of me, and the seemingly wise shun me.

I do not know what they look like. I cannot tell you the color of their skin, their eyes, or their hair. I have no way of knowing how ugly or good looking they are, or what dress they wear.

To me they are the same. People - all the same. Short; tall, strong, weak, muscular, skinny; I do not know. They are all very similar to me. I only know that they are human. I am not prejudiced nor am I racial.

There are dogs that bark. I am told that they bite as well. I hear them. I sometimes smell them near me and hear them breathing. I have heard of their foul breath and I am glad they do not come too close.

Birds are a thing of the air. They sing beautifully. I sometimes hear their wings flapping hard as they take flight. But I have never seen them fly.

Roosters crow and make a fuss in the mornings. But as the creatures begin to wake up and greet the morning, what beautiful sounds they make.

I hear that the rising of the sun is absolutely gorgeous. How beautiful? I would truly love to know! Also they tell me that the dawn is just as spectacular if not even more so.

Have you heard the chickens when they have laid their eggs? Oh, the ruckus.

One thing I love though is to hear children chatting together. They have so much to say. Always cheerful and going on; always laughing over something! And sometimes they are loud, but I can put up with that.

It would be a marvel if adults would return to that. Oh, if grown-ups were like children! What a different world we would live in. No more cussing and complaining. No more talking about the neighbors and the friend who was once so close.

Oh, I hear it all. They hang around and go on and on. I might have a defect, but boy I do have good ears.

Little ones, believe me, can be such fun! Yea, they may call me names sometimes, but they mean nothing by it. They are just having a good time.

Adults? No! If they call you something, duck! You do not know how high it is flying and how hard it will hit.

Have you ever listened to a child singing to the world? I have. The world is his stage, and creation, his audience. Nothing means anything, but his singing is everything. To him, his tranquil existence, full of joy and freedom will never cease.

I guess . . . I just love children. They make me happy. Do you love children? You should. They are wonderful. They are the best!

One type of people who come close to being like little ones, are shepherds. They come down the street a-yelling. You would think those poor sheep didn't have parents; that they were kind of thrown out on the streets as if they had no value.

Oh, shepherds carry on. How they do go on! They yell and scream and slap their staffs on the road, "Get back in there you stupid sheep!"

You should hear them sometimes!

I have been hit by a rock once or twice. I am not sure if it was the "stupid sheep" or the "wise keeper." Neither one have said sorry. But, it is life I guess.

Tell me something. Why do people have to beat their animals? The poor beasts work for them all day long!

They lug heavy loads on their backs day after day for these apparently intelligent keepers. They pull overloaded carts up and down steep roads and hills while they bake in the sun and heat. They are hardly offered water on the way, are hungry most of the time, and cannot stop for anything.

To stop is to rob their *supposedly suffering* master from earning a full day's wage. But, he doesn't carry the load on his back, or pull the heavy cart!

I have heard the slap of rods on the backs of these wretched creatures that are born to carry burdens. Where is the conscience of these individuals who are so religious, so pious and oh, such "holier-than-thou" temple frequenters?

Sometimes I wish I had a whip in my hand, and the goon was standing close; or, that the situation was turned around; that he was the beast and the beast was him.

I guess it all pertains to life. It all adds to our experiences. Though there are many experiences that I wish I have not had to endure.

Take my blindness for example. I cannot tell what you look like. I cannot tell you that you are beautiful. Then I would be lying. I really don't know. But I guess that if I said that you have inner beauty that would likely be the truth. I do not need to see you to know that you are beautiful on the inside.

Perhaps I have a better sense of inner beauty than most people, since I cannot tell what you look like. I am not biased therefore, the reason being that I do not see your outward beauty. I guess then, that in this way I have an advantage.

However, there are other points too. I do not know what it looks like when the sun is rising or when it is going down.

As parents behold the face of a little angel held in his mother's arms, they think he is the most beautiful and wonderful being in the whole world. I have no clue what that is like!

A little song bird sits in the branches. He sings his little heart out. His song is so melodious and delicious, it blesses my soul. But . . . how I wish I could consider its splendor with seeing eyes. If only I could see its feathers fluff, and its mouth move at every syllable and note.

Ah . . . to be able to see. It is my greatest desire.

I may never see. Born with this disability, and having lived with it all my life, one might think that this is normal. To a degree it is. Oh, to have what others take for granted!

To see, to hear, to walk, to talk, to speak, to do all the things that a perfectly healthy body is capable of doing, is normal. Being blind to me is not normal. I lack something. You can see, but I can't. And so, I have wished that somehow, somewhere along life's path, by some miracle, perhaps I would see.

I have heard not so long ago that such miracles are happening around these areas. There seems to be a great prophet performing healings of all kinds. He has even cast out demons from people.

I wonder what that is all about. I have only heard about these manifestations. I have never seen them myself.

This great man has even raised the dead, so they tell me. I am not sure if that is one of those housewives' tales! However, if he is casting out demons and causing the lame to walk, the deaf to hear, the dumb to speak, and even the blind eyes to see, then he should be able to also raise the dead.

I wish that this man would come to our city!

They call him Jesus the Christ. He was born in Bethlehem, but he lived in Nazareth. And so they also call Him Jesus of Nazareth. If He ever comes our way, boy, I hope that he can do something for me.

It's been many long years, and it would be nice to have a change. Every day, the same routine: being led to the corner, having lunch brought to me, and then being picked up at evening time. This melancholy way of living is just not doing it for me any longer. I need a change!

Early One Day

"Thank you Joel. See you at lunch hour."

"Bye Uncle. See you later."

"Don't forget to bring me a piece of that cake your Mom made yesterday. That was delicious."

"I won't Uncle. See you later." Joel scampers away.

Joel is a good boy. Ever since he has been old enough, he has walked me to the corner. Then at dusk he returns to get me. Or, if I needed to, I would send word home, and someone would come and take me back.

The air is sweet this morning. It smells clean. There was a nice shower in the wee hours of the morning and it has left everything nice and fresh. It is all dry now, so sitting down in my regular spot won't be a bother.

I hope that I do better than yesterday. It seems that every one spent everything they had on the Sabbath. It just trickled in.

Late Afternoon Sometime

The boy hasn't arrived yet. He should be here soon though. It is going to be dark in a little while.

I have done well today, much better than yesterday.

People seem to be more giving for some reason.

"What's that? Hey . . . Hey, John! What is that racket? Where is it coming from?"

"There is a crowd of people coming down the street. They are headed this way. What a lot of people! I'll go see what all the commotion is about."

"It's Jesus! It is Jesus!" John exclaimed, huffing and puffing. He ran all the way back to tell me what was happening. He was so excited that the words seem to run together.

"I can't hear you! There is too much noise!"

Putting his mouth to my ear he screamed, "It is Jesus the Healer!"

"Jesus, the Healer? You mean He is here?"

"Yes, Bartimaeus! He is here! That's Him passing by right now. Oh, I forget- you can't see."

"Jesus! Jesus! Son of David! Have mercy on me!"

"Be quiet! Leave him alone!" Someone shouted at me. It wasn't John.

"Jesus! Son of David, have mercy on me!" Jesus is here. I can't stop now. I have been waiting all my life for this.

"What do you want with him? Stop shouting you blind bat! The man is too busy. He doesn't have time for you."

"Son of David, have mercy on me! Jesus . . ."

"It's okay. He has asked for you to come to him. Come, I will help you to Jesus."

I do not need this coat anymore. It's only keeping me back. There . . . I am free of it.

"Let's go quickly. Take me to Him, please."

"Give way, make space! Let us through! Jesus is waiting for this man."

"Here he is Lord."

"Thank you, Peter." "What would you like me to do for you?"

"I want to see, Lord!"

"Go on then, you have what you ask for because of your faith."

> "And they came to Jericho: and as He went out of Jericho with His disciples and a great number of people, blind Bartimaeus, the son of Timaeus, sat by the highway side begging. And when he heard that it was Jesus of Nazareth, he began to cry out, and say, Jesus, thou son of David, have mercy on me. And many charged him that he should hold his peace: but he cried the more a great deal, Thou son of David, have mercy on me. And many charged him that he should hold his peace: but he cried the more a

great deal, Thou son of David, have mercy on me. And Jesus stood still, and commanded him to be called. And they call the blind man, saying unto him, be of good comfort, rise; he calleth thee. And he, casting away his garment, rose, and came to Jesus. And Jesus answered and said unto him, what wilt thou that I should do unto thee? The blind man said unto him, Lord, that I might receive my sight. And Jesus said unto him, Go thy way; thy faith hath made thee whole. And immediately he received his sight, and followed Jesus in the way." Mark 10:46–52

The Cloak

Representing the past; full of sadness, loneliness and despair, this cloak had to be thrown off. It was symbolic of his past. It embodied old feelings of brokenness, darkness, loneliness, shame, failure, doubts and fear, discouragement and hindrance.

Can you picture Bartimaeus returning to the same corner after receiving his sight? Sitting down in his usual spot and continuing his old trade of begging? Can you imagine him wearing the same filthy, foul, tattered old cloak, covering himself just the same way as he did before?

Can you see him in your mind's eye doing all of that? Can you imagine the scene as people pass by and notice him there? What would they be thinking?

No one in their right mind would go back to a corner such as that one! Nor throw on a grimy old cloak that they once used while blind and a beggar.

You wouldn't return to such a life style! Not in this life or in any other!

In your past life is such a cloak of poverty, shame, failure, disability of one form or another. It represents beggarly mentality, doubts and fears, blindness, low self-esteem, remorse, pride, hate, malice, and unforgiveness. And it must be cast aside!

If you were not to chuck that cloak of your past, but sit in the same old corner of your life, continue to do the same old things you used to do, you would think the same way, make similar mistakes, and earn the same old wages.

You would therefore have returned to your former blind and beggarly state.

Be wise and cast off that cloak. Set it out for the garbage truck!

Live in the new life that Christ has given to you. Stick with the new sight that you have received and the new wages of "eternal life." Walk in the glorious bright and open future that you have received.

You have had enough of a lifetime of blindness. Do not go back to it! You have had enough of a lifetime of dust and dirt, shame and cruelty. Hurl the past away! Take it to the fire heap and burn it. You have better wages now.

You see better today. There is more beauty to behold, more peace to be gained, and much laughter to be heard. And there is greater abundance of joy to experience.

The birds are more beautiful than ever before. The smile on a baby's face is awesome. The flowers, trees, butterflies, bees, and even the old smelly dogs are an amazing sight to behold. Everything is now so magnificent!

Do you still want to go back to where and what you were?

Go with Bartimaeus. Follow Jesus.

Bartimaeus threw off from himself a cloak that stood for all that was poverty and shame in his life. He had no plans of returning to the past. To Bartimaeus, his past was dead. He had received new life. *Not just a new lease on life, but New Life!* He followed Jesus.

It took courage, faith, perseverance and determination to do what Bartimaeus did. And because of it he received the greatest thing that he ever desired; his sight.

Bartimaeus got up from the ground. He left behind the low, broken, filthy, degrading and empty place in life, where he was seated. He rose up from degradation to exaltation. Leaving shame, failure, and his beggarly state behind, He ascended to become prosperous. He lifted up off the cushion of nothingness to sit on a throne in the

Kingdom of God.

You can do the same! Perhaps you have already done the equivalent.

Leaving all that was he gained, that which is, and all that is to come. He exchanged the old for the new.

He became what he wasn't; he gained what he didn't have; he rose to an altitude that he never dreamt of and to a position he had only hoped for. He turned toward an upward ascent when he was in a downward spiral. He chose wisely. His decision was quick and to the point. He profited!

When you choose like Bratimaeus who had nothing, but gained everything, you will also profit like he did.

God Responds To Faith

"But unto the Son he saith, Thy throne, O God, is for ever and ever: a sceptre of righteousness is the sceptre of thy kingdom." Hebrew 1:8

Righteousness is yours. You do not have to beg for it or work for it. You were previously given it. *You already have it.* You are righteousness in Christ.

You already have. You only need to believe that you do. God's word is true and forever will be. You were made the righteousness of God the moment that you received Christ as your Lord and Savior.

Bartimaeus had a greater mountain to climb. His one desire was not fulfilled all his life. He had to believe, determine, persevere and fight off the gainsayers who told him to shut up. He rose above it all and gained victory.

> "For what saith the scripture? Abraham believed God, and it was counted unto him for righteousness. But to him that worketh not, but believeth on him that justifieth the ungodly, his faith is counted for righteousness." Romans 4:3, 5

The blind man cast off a cloak that typified a past of death and nothingness to receive a new covering in Christ. When he answered the call of Jesus and walked toward Him, He had already won.

As you get up by faith from where you are seated in life, and walk in the righteousness of God, absolutely nothing can defeat you.

This cloak represents everything that is past in your life: sin, shame, fear, low self-esteem, anger, frustration, curses, habits, bondages, narrow mindedness, doubts, regrets, hopelessness, fear of failure, . . . you can fill in the rest!

All that is of your past is held in that cloak. Have you cast it off as yet?

After throwing off his cloak, Bartimaeus walked toward Jesus. That walk was a journey of victory, celebration and gladness of heart. It embraced an abundance of forgiveness, grace, mercy, joy, and immeasurable peace.

Hurl your past aside and walk toward Jesus. You will walk forever in the victory that is already yours.

Set that boat of your past afloat! Cut its moorings. Take a ride on the ship that is sailing Heaven's way. Get on board the flight that is only going in one direction, and that is in the way of *victory*.

As the blind man reached Jesus he was asked, "What do you want me to do for you?"

You too will be asked the same question.

Bartimaeus screamed out in faith. He was heard and in turn was sent for by the Master, who demanded, "Bring him here!"

When you throw away your past of doubts and fear and call in faith, you will also hear the same question, "What do you want me to do for you?"

Note clearly: Jesus did not ask the man about his past. He did not inquire of him as to why he left his coat behind. He did not demand to know how much time he spent at the Temple that week. Nor did he question him as to how much he prayed. He only asked him what he wanted.

God responds to faith. It is faith that moves God's hands to provide our wants and needs.

> "Jesus said unto him, if thou canst believe, *all things*

are possible to him that believeth." Mark 9:23

"Therefore I say unto you, what things soever ye desire, when ye pray, *believe* that ye receive them, and ye shall have them." Mark 11:24

"Verily, verily, I say unto you, he that *believeth* on me, the works that I do shall he do also; and greater works than these shall he do; because I go unto my Father." John 14:12

"Jesus saith unto him, go thy way; thy son liveth. And the man *believed* the word that Jesus had spoken unto him, and he went his way. So the father knew that it was at the same hour, in which Jesus said unto him, Thy son liveth: and himself believed, and his whole house." John 4:50, 53

Bartimaeus' response was, "I would like to see, Lord." If Jesus asked you today, "What do you want me to do for you?" What would be your response?

"Go your way your faith has made you whole," is what you will hear Jesus say to you.

"For we walk by faith, not by sight:"

2nd Corinthians 5:7.

The blind man became a new man; a seeing man, a joyful man; a man with a new future.

Righteousness is received by faith. The fact of the matter is that you were established in righteousness in Christ. The question is; are you walking in that righteousness?

"For if by one man's offence death reigned by one; much more they which receive abundance of grace and of the *gift of righteousness* shall reign in life by one, Jesus Christ." Romans 5:17

Therefore you are to reign in your life through the life of Christ that is in you. And that life in Christ is righteousness.

> "For therein is the righteousness of God revealed from faith to faith: as it is written, the just shall *live by faith.* Even *the righteousness of God which is by faith of Jesus Christ unto all and upon all them that believe*: for there is no difference: What shall we say then? That the Gentiles, which followed not after righteousness, have attained to righteousness, even the righteousness which is of faith." Romans 1:17; 3:22; 9:30

The very moment that Bartimaeus tossed away the cloak of his past, he began a new walk. His walk started in faith as He called out to Jesus. It continued in faith as he walked to the Master, and I believe that it finished in faith after Jesus left Jericho.

The once blind man never picked up the cloak and wore it again, nor did he ever again sit in the familiar spot to beg. He now had what he always desired. He knew one thing without an ounce of doubt; God provides. He hears and responds to the call of faith.

The cloak, which was a consciousness of everything that is evil: sin and shame; doubt and fear; rejection and failure; hurt and pain, poverty and wantonness, was cast down; left behind forever.

Throw yours to the ground! Stomp on it and grind it into the dirt. Dig a deep hole and bury it. Never return to it. Forever forget it. Turn and walk away from it. Head toward Jesus and victory: new life; everlasting joy and gladness, peace and happiness, and abundance of grace and pardon await you. God has already made you His righteousness in Christ.

It is the same as a blind man receiving sight. He is no longer blind. He will never again wonder what a baby's smile looks like. Nor will he wonder what a song bird appears like in the branches of a tree, as he makes joyful melody to the world around it. This new Bartimaeus will never walk in blindness again. How about you?

Jesus said to him, "Go, you have received what you asked for by your faith."

The connection to your past–the cloak of everything unrighteous- discard it. Go to Jesus and pick up a new life: *the righteousness of God.*

"And that ye *put on the new man, which after God is created in righteousness and true holiness.*" Ephesians 4:24

When He said that you were made the righteousness of

God, He didn't mean that you were *going* to be made the righteousness of God. It is already done. The very moment that you accepted Christ Jesus as your Lord and Savior you received the gift of righteousness.

Now, all that is left for you to do is exist in that very state that you are in - righteous state.

You should by no means walk as an unrighteous person ever again. Not unless you turn back to sin and continue to live in it.

However, if you fall into sin, but repent from your heart over it, you will be forgiven and washed with the blood of Jesus. You will be cleansed of all unrighteousness (sin) and have fellowship with the Lord restored to you.

What is left when all unrighteousness is removed? That's right, *righteousness!* Live in it.

> "And if Christ be in you, the body is dead because of sin; but *the Spirit is life* because of righteousness." Romans 8:10

> "For they being ignorant of God's righteousness, and going about to establish their own righteousness, have not submitted themselves unto the righteousness of God. For Christ is the end of the law for righteousness to every one that believeth." Romans 10:3, 4

> "For the kingdom of God is not meat and drink; but righteousness, and peace, and joy

in the Holy Ghost." Romans 14:17

"I do not frustrate the grace of God: for if righteousness come by the law, then Christ is dead in vain." Galatians 2:21

Chapter 10

GRACE, ISN'T IT AMAZING?

Light has no brilliance, life has no fullness, and love has no greatness like God's. The power and force of His light, His life, and His love are unmatchable, unfathomable and indescribable.

Righteousness fills all in all. Goodness, mercy and grace are unaccountable. The richness of His Presence is beyond description. And the force of His glory is unimaginable.

Full of glory, full of grace, overflowing with compassion and love, and pouring out of Him and from Him, life in magnificent completeness.

Regal in majesty supreme, crowned with glory and abundance of grace, and existing in power of pure perfection.

In His presence is fullness of joy and peace that passes understanding. Gladness of heart overwhelms you. You are carried off into its' realm as if in a dream. Light as a feather, you float on air in His awesome presence.

You are engulfed in the oneness of God. You have been pulled into and made a part of that oneness; into the very existence of the Trinity: the Godhead. You were made to share in His divine nature. Oh, no, you are not God! But, you share His divine nature and you exist in and through Him.

From Him pours into you that *life*, that *love*, and that *light* that is unmatchable, unfathomable and indescribable.

You are saturated and are overflowing throughout whatever place you may be. You carry that same presence everywhere you go; into whatever place, and into whatever situation. You stand correct, without flaw. Clean, pure, holy, true, full of power and anointing. There is no space between you and God. You are one with Him in Christ.

All the power, strength, wisdom, and the very nature of God, are within you. Every evidence of God's existence, His anointing, and His miracle power are part of you now. You spill over with peace that passes understanding. You experience joy unspeakable and full of glory.

You are brimming with goodness, laughter and gladness. Glory shines all around, and you are full of confidence. Faith rises from within and floods your soul.

This glory land, this heaven; this is living in the presence of Almighty God!

Judgment was passed; you are Justified.

Like a common criminal you were scornfully accused and had your life set out before everyone. You were ready to accept any punishment that would have been handed to you. You were expecting eternal damnation.

But, Grace, isn't it amazing?

You stand before the Maker of your soul and His love bathes you. You cannot, but, want to scream out with the ecstatic feeling of great joy that is overwhelming your soul.

Awe is not sufficient to express the moment; *marvelous* is too little a word, and *great* is but weak to describe what you are feeling.

This is Father God before your very eyes. Jesus, your Lord and Savior is the One smiling back at you.

Heaven was described to you, but never like this. No one ever told you that experiencing the presence of God would be this way. Not this awesome, not this great and marvelous!

Oh, the love that pours into and through your soul, the joy and thrill of salvation, the spectacular beauty of faith, and the majesty of His Presence. None can tell how beautiful, how marvelous, how perfect. God your Father, Jesus Christ your Lord, beholding you with love that surpasses all imagination and understanding.

You are as light as a feather. Although your feet are on the ground, they are not carrying you. You are adrift in the majesty of love supreme, and swimming in tranquility and peace that passes all understanding.

How sweet, how glorious is the thought that you have arrived. This is it! This is what your Master died for. This is why He came to the earth.

Oh, the awesome greatness of the act of love that bridges mankind to his Creator and God. Jesus accomplished it! He paid in full the debt for your every sin. Now you are free!

How blessed it is to be in the presence of Almighty God.

Once you thought how difficult it would be; how frightening. But here you are in God's Presence. You are accepted, pardoned, washed in Christ's blood, and have been made God's righteousness. You are a new creation.

Now you recognize what it is to be holy, to be a king and a priest. You feel His purity in and through you. You recognize without a shadow of a doubt that you can approach your Father God anytime as a priest. And you realize that you reign and rule with Christ on the earth.

This is what it is to be one with Jesus. His power, His grace, His beauty, His anointing, His wisdom, His righteousness; all that is Jesus is in you. All the authority that

Christ has on the earth . . . you have in His name.

What a feeling! How can you describe it? It is not easy. If only you could understand. But to understand is to experience. To experience the presence of God is to surrender to His love. And to surrender to His love is to accept His act of love; Christ crucified and resurrected in your stead.

Accepting His act of love is to receive Christ as your personal Savior and Lord. And to receive Christ is to be recreated in righteousness and God's divine nature.

Having been recreated in your spirit and having God's divine nature is to experience His presence. For then, in you dwells Holy Spirit who raised Christ from the dead and who shall transform you from the inside out day by day. And it is He who facilitates intimacy between you and your Heavenly Father.

Now you have rest, because "there is therefore now no condemnation since you are in Christ." Finally, you understand the meaning of these words. You are experiencing justification. You are justified and basking in the presence of Almighty God; overshadowed by His glory and infinite beauty.

You stand before your King in His righteousness. God looks at you and sees His own reflection. He sees His own light shining back at Him. This has been His working; His creative work, His act of making you blameless. You are accepted in the Beloved.

There cannot be greater perfection than this. This is as perfect as it will ever get here on the earth. That is why if you died right now you would go straight to Heaven. To be absent from the body is to be present with the Lord.

God your Father made this possible by making you His righteousness; a new creation, holy and acceptable.

Righteousness doesn't grow on you, nor does it come because of any of your good works. You have it and that is it. As Jesus is the only begotten Son of God the Father, so you too have become a son of God. That doesn't change. In the same way, being God's righteousness doesn't change.

Full of the nature of Love you are now able to love as He loves. You have the mind of Christ. You can do all things because He strengthens you and works in and through you to fulfill His will. And He is happy and pleased to do it.

Righteousness is not a result of good works. It doesn't come out from you. It comes from God and it is a direct result of an act of God. He made you righteousness, and now you can have intimate relationship with Him.

He recreated you to have righteousness so that you might fellowship with Him, who is righteous. He is your righteousness. You remain forever justified in Christ as long as you continue in Him.

Let Us Recap

"God's WORD is a mirror. If you look into it long enough, you will see yourself."

You are just, because you were justified by God. You were declared to be justified, and were made God's righteousness. And you live by faith. Not just by your faith, but by Christ's faith.

> Galatians 2:20, "I am crucified with Christ: neverthless I live; yet not I, but Christ liveth in me: and the life which I now live in the flesh *I live by the faith of the Son of God*, who loved me, and gave himself for me."
>
> Romans 3:26, "To declare, I say, at this time his righteousness: that he might be just, and *the justifi er of him which believeth in Jesus*."
>
> Hebrews 10:38, "Now the just shall live by faith . . ."
>
> Luke 7:50, "And he said to the woman, *Thy faith hath saved thee*; go in peace."
>
> Luke 17:19, "And he said unto him, Arise, go thy way: *thy faith hath made thee whole*."
>
> Romans 3:28, "Therefore we conclude that *a man is justified by faith* without the deeds of the law."
>
> Hebrews 11:6, "But without faith it is impossible to please him: for he that cometh

> to God must believe that he is, and that he is a rewarder of them that diligently seek him."

Now, because you were justified you have peace that passes all understanding. It is not something that you should be pleading with God for, but thanking Him for.

> Romans 5:1, 2 "Therefore being justified by faith, we have peace with God through our Lord Jesus Christ: By whom also we have access by faith into this grace wherein we stand, and rejoice in hope of the glory of God."

> Isaiah 32:17, "And the work of righteousness shall be peace; and the effect of righteousness quietness and assurance for ever."

You have been recreated in your spirit in the image and likeness of Christ. You are *not going to be* in His image and likeness, you already are. One day you will be changed in a twinkling of an eye and will be caught up to meet Him in the air, if you are still here on the earth when He comes.

You will be changed from mortality to immortality. But, you already have His image and likeness in your spirit. You are constantly being transformed from glory to glory by Holy Spirit in likeness of Christ's speech, walk and action.

Colossians 3:10, "And *have put on the new man*, which is renewed in knowledge after the image of him that created him:"

2nd Corinthians 5:17, "Therefore if any man be in Christ, he is a *new creature*: old things are passed away; behold, all things are become new."

2nd Corinthians 3:18, "But we all, with open face beholding as in a glass the glory of the Lord, are changed into *the same image* from glory to glory, even as by the Spirit of the Lord."

2nd Corinthians 4:4, "In whom the god of this world hath blinded the minds of them which believe not, lest the light of the glorious gospel of *Christ, who is the image of God,* should shine unto them."

Philippians 3:21, "Who shall change our *vile body,* that it may be fashioned like unto his *glorious body,* according to the working whereby he is able even to subdue all things unto himself."

You are God's righteousness. You were recreated in your spirit to be God's righteousness.

2nd Corinthians 5:21, "For he hath made him to be sin for us, who knew no sin; that we might be made *the righteousness of God* in him (Christ)."

Ephesians 4:24, "And that ye put on *the new man,* which after God is *created in righteousness* and true holiness."

Psalm 24:5 "*He shall receive* the blessing from the lord, *and righteousness* from the God of his salvation."

Philippians 3:9, "And be found in him, not having mine own righteousness, which is of the law, but that which is through the faith of Christ, *the righteousness which is of God* by faith:"

1st Corinthians 1:30, "But of him are ye in Christ Jesus, who of God is made unto us wisdom, and *righteousness*, and *sanctification*, and *redemption*:"

Romans 14:17, "For *the kingdom of God* is not meat and drink; but *righteousness*, and peace, and joy in the Holy Ghost."

You received God's righteousness by faith and because of His grace. God's righteousness is a gift to you. You do not have to do anything for it, but accept it as you would any gift.

Romans 3:22, "Even the righteousness of God which is by faith of Jesus Christ unto all and upon all them that believe: for there is no difference:"

Romans 5:17, 18 "For if by one man's offence death reigned by one; much more they which *receive abundance of grace* and of

> *the gift of righteousness* shall reign in life by one, Jesus Christ.)Therefore as by the offence of one judgment came upon all men to condemnation; even so by the righteousness of one *the free gift* came upon all men unto justification of life."

> Isaiah 54:17, "No weapon that is formed against thee shall prosper; and every tongue that shall rise against thee in judgment thou shalt condemn. This is the heritage of the servants of the lord, *and their righteousness is of me*, saith the lord."

You became the righteousness of God because you were washed in the blood of Jesus Christ when you received Him as your Lord and Savior.

> Revelations 1:5, "And from Jesus Christ, who is the faithful witness, and the first begotten of the dead, and the prince of the kings of the earth. Unto him that loved us, and washed us from our sins in his own blood."

> Romans 10:9, 10 "That if thou shalt confess with thy mouth the Lord Jesus, and shalt believe in thine heart that God hath raised him from the dead, thou shalt be saved. For with the heart man *believeth unto righteousness*; and with the mouth confession is made unto salvation."

> Hebrews 9:12, "Neither by the blood of

> goats and calves, but *by his own blood* he entered in once into the holy place, having *obtained eternal redemption for us.*"

You were once a partaker of the nature of wrath or sin and of Satan. You now share in God's divine nature.

> John 9:34, "They answered and said unto him, Thou wast altogether born in sins (sin-Satan's nature), and dost thou teach us? And they cast him out."

> Ephesians 2:3, "Among whom also we all had our conversation in times past in the lusts of our flesh, fulfilling the desires of the flesh and of the mind; *and were by nature the children of wrath*, even as others."

> 2nd Peter 1:4, "Whereby are given unto us exceeding great and precious promises: that by these ye might be *partakers of the divine nature*, having escaped the corruption that is in the world through lust."

> John 14:20, "At that day ye shall know that I am in my Father, and ye in me, and I in you."

> 1st John 3:10, "In this the children of God are manifest, and the children of the devil . . ."

When God looks upon you He sees His righteousness, He sees Jesus. You are accepted by God in Christ the Beloved.

> Psalm 11:7, "For the righteous lord loveth

righteousness; his countenance doth *behold the upright* (that is you-righteous.)"

> Ephesians 1:4, 6, "According as he hath *chosen us in him* before the foundation of the world, that we should be holy and without blame *before him in love*: To the praise of the glory of his grace, wherein *he hath made us accepted in the beloved* (Christ)."

> Colossians 1:21, 22, "And you, that were sometime alienated and enemies in your mind by wicked works, yet now hath he reconciled in the body of his flesh through death, to *present you holy* and unblameable and unreproveable *in his sight*:"

You are complete in Christ and can do all things in His strength because He strengthens you. Not only does He strengthen you, He works in and through you. You do not have to reach a certain altitude for Him or measure up. You are complete in Him.

> Colossians 2:10, "And *ye are complete in him*, which is the head of all principality and power:"

> Philippians 4:13, "I can do all things through Christ which strengtheneth me."

> Philippians 2:13, "For it is God which worketh in you both to will and to do of his good pleasure."

You were made an heir of God in Christ. Everything that is Christ's is yours.

> Titus 3:7, "That being justified by his grace, *we should be made heirs* according to the hope of eternal life."
>
> Romans 8:17 "And if children, then heirs; heirs of God, and joint-heirs with Christ; if so be that we suffer with him, that we may be also glorified together."
>
> Galatians 3:29, "And if ye be Christ's, then are ye Abraham's seed, and heirs according to the promise."

You are established in righteousness.

> Isaiah 45:24, "Surely, shall one say, in the lord have I righteousness and strength:"
>
> Isaiah 54:14, "In righteousness shalt thou be established: thou shalt be far from oppression; for thou shalt not fear: and from terror; for it shall not come near thee."
>
> Romans 8:10, "And if Christ be in you, the body is dead because of sin; but the Spirit is life because of righteousness."
>
> Ephesians 6:14, "Stand therefore, having your loins girt about with truth, and having on the breastplate of righteousness;"

You were made a king and a priest to rule on this earth *now* through Christ, and to worship and serve Him as a priest. You represent Him on this earth. As He is–in all power and anointing - so are you on the earth.

> Revelations 1:6, "And hath made us kings and priests unto God and his Father; to him be glory and dominion for ever and ever. Amen."
>
> Revelations 5:10, "And hast made us unto our God kings and priests: and we shall reign on the earth."
>
> 1st John 4:17, "Herein is our love made perfect, that we may have boldness in the day of judgment: because *as he is, so are we in this world.*"

You are chosen, holy and acceptable, without blame in Christ, royal, peculiar and well loved.

> 1st Peter 1:16, "Because it is written, Be ye holy; for I am holy."
>
> Ephesians 1:4, "According as he hath *chosen us in him* before the foundation of the world, that we should be holy and without blame before him in love:"
>
> Colossians 3:12, "Put on therefore, as the elect of God, *holy and beloved*, bowels of mercies, kindness, humbleness of mind,

meekness, longsuffering;"

1st Peter 2:5, "Ye also, as lively stones, are built up a spiritual house, an *holy priesthood,* to offer up spiritual sacrifices, acceptable to God by Jesus Christ."

1st Peter 2:9, "But ye are a chosen generation, a *royal priesthood,* an holy nation, a *peculiar* people; that ye should shew forth the praises of him who hath called you out of darkness into his marvellous light;"

You are a saint. You are not going to be a saint when you die if you are not already one now.

Romans 1:7, "To all that be in Rome, beloved of God, called to be saints: Grace to you and peace from God our Father, and the Lord Jesus Christ."

Romans 8:27, "And he that searcheth the hearts knoweth what is the mind of the Spirit, because he maketh intercession for *the saints* according to the will of God."

1st Corinthians 1:2, "Unto the church of God which is at Corinth, to *them that are sanctified in Christ Jesus, called to be saints*, with all that in every place call upon the name of Jesus Christ our Lord, both their's and our's:"

Philippians 1:1, "Paul and Timotheus, the

> servants of Jesus Christ, to *all the saints in Christ Jesus* which are at Philippi, with the bishops and deacons:"

You have the power that Christ gave to His disciples. You are one with Him, and greater is He in you than the devil in the world. Therefore you can do the works that He did, and even greater works, as Jesus said you would do.

> Matthew 28:18, "And Jesus came and spake unto them, saying, *All power is given unto me in heaven and in earth.*"

> Luke 10:19, "Behold, *I give unto you power* to tread on serpents and scorpions, and over all the power of the enemy: and nothing shall by any means hurt you."

> John 14:12, "Verily, verily, I say unto you, He that believeth on me, the works that I do shall he do also; and greater works than these shall he do; because I go unto my Father."

> 1st John 4:4, "Ye are of God, little children, and have overcome them: because *greater is he that is in you, than he that is in the world.*"

Your fellowship with God has been restored and you are able to enter into His throne room; into His presence, and fellowship with Him at any time you please.

> Hebrews 10:19, 20 "Having therefore, brethren, *boldness to enter* into the holiest by

the blood of Jesus, By a new and living way, which he hath consecrated for us, through the veil, that is to say, his flesh;"

Hebrews 4:16, "Let us therefore *come boldly unto the throne of grace*, that we may obtain mercy, and find grace to help in time of need."

The time has come, and the hour is now. Love the Lord your God with all your heart and with all your strength. Remember, it is Holy Spirit in you doing it all.

"I have preached righteousness in the great congregation: lo, I have not refrained my lips, o lord, thou knowest. I have not hid thy righteousness within my heart; I have declared thy faithfulness and thy salvation: I have not concealed thy lovingkindness and thy truth from the great congregation." Psalm 40: 9, 10

2 Timothy 3:16, "*All scripture is given by inspiration of God*, and is profitable for doctrine, for reproof, for correction, *for instruction in righteousness:*"

So believe, receive and be forever blessed!

Philippians 1:6, "Being confident of this very thing, that he which hath begun a good work in you will perform it until the day of Jesus Christ:"

Like Paul, I too am confident that He who has begun a good work in you will complete it. Amen!

> "Now the God of peace, that brought again from the dead our Lord Jesus, that great shepherd of the sheep, through the blood of the everlasting covenant, make you perfect in every good work to do his will, working in you that which is well pleasing in his sight, through Jesus Christ; to whom be glory for ever and ever. Amen." Hebrews 13:20, 21

Has, What You Weren't Told About Righteousness made a difference in your life? Did it do anything for you at all? Please tell us. Write to us at the address below, or send an email. Pastor Ramiah would love to hear what the Lord has done for you.

You may find these other books, life changing as well:

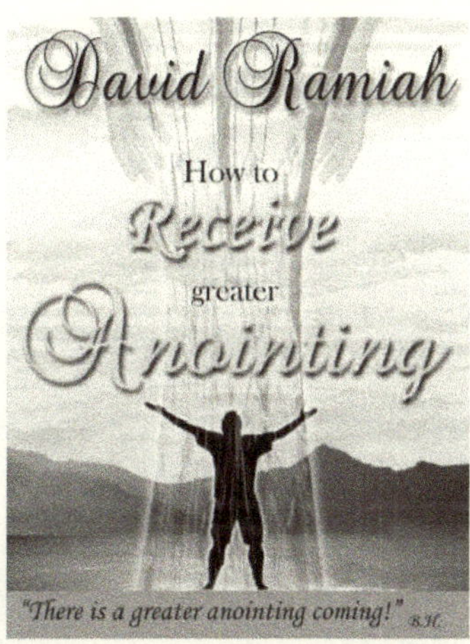

You can quickly and easily order any of these books on our website.

www.ChristExaltedMinistries.com
mail@ChristExaltedMinistries.com
Christ Exalted Ministries
22-90 Signet Drive,
Toronto, Ontario, M9L 1T5

We also have a ***testimony*** section in our website where your *personal testimony* could be placed. Check out the website.

www.ingramcontent.com/pod-product-compliance
Lightning Source LLC
Chambersburg PA
CBHW021054090426
42738CB00006B/334

* 9 7 8 0 9 7 3 3 2 4 7 8 5 *